SHOULD DRUGS BE LEGALIZED

**Also by
Susan Neiburg Terkel**

*Abortion:
Facing the Issues*

SHOULD DRUGS BE LEGALIZED

SUSAN NEIBURG TERKEL

FRANKLIN WATTS
NEW YORK/LONDON/TORONTO/SYDNEY/1990

Charts by Vantage Art

Library of Congress Cataloging-in-Publication Data
Terkel, Susan Neiburg.
Should drugs be legalized? / by Susan Neiburg Terkel.
p.   cm.
Includes bibliographical references.
Summary: Discusses the history of drug laws in the United States
and examines the possibilities of drug legalization.
ISBN 0-531-15182-4 — ISBN 0-531-10944-5 (lib. bdg.)
1. Narcotic laws—United States—Juvenile literature.
2. Decriminalization—United States—Juvenile literature.
3. Narcotics, Control of—United States—Juvenile literature.
[1. Narcotic laws.   2. Narcotics, Control of.]   I. Title.
KF3890.Z9T47   1990
363.4'5'0973—dc20   90-32902   CIP AC

CONTENTS

This book is dedicated to my aunt and uncle,
Naomi and Jerome Burstein

SHOULD DRUGS BE LEGALIZED

ACKNOWLEDGMENTS

Gratitude goes to my editor, Iris Rosoff; to my agent, Andrea Brown; and to the experts who read my manuscript and helped me understand the issue: David Courtwright, Ph.D., Rick Hanna, William Kroman, Evelyn Sabino, Joseph Sabino, and Kathryn Wakeling.

Appreciation also goes to Melvyn Durchslag, Brooke Kowalski, Pat Raudins, Margie Origlio, Roy Scherer, and Deanne Smierciak. Special appreciation goes to my husband, Larry, and my children, Ari, Marni, and David, for listening to endless drafts and for giving me so much encouragement.

1

PROPHECIES OF CHANGE

Sisyphus was a Greek god whose task it was to roll a huge rock up a mountain. Every time Sisyphus neared the summit, the rock rolled down again. Still, he persisted, hoping that eventually he would succeed.

Like Sisyphus, our government has been toiling at a task. For more than seventy-five years, we have rolled the rock of drug prohibition up the mountain of drug abuse. Like Sisyphus, we have not yet succeeded. Like him, too, we try again and again.

Each year, the United States resolves to win the war on drugs. We spend billions more on law enforcement. We wipe out more illegal crops, destroy more illegal laboratories, and seize more illegal drugs. We arrest, convict, and punish more drug criminals. We stiffen the fines and lengthen the sentences.

And that's not all. We try to stop the demand for drugs. Through educational programs like "Just Say No," we try to convince people how harmful drugs are. Through treatment, we try to get people off drugs.

Despite our efforts, more than fourteen million Americans use illegal drugs regularly. They are getting the drugs and not getting the message. Or else, they are choosing to ignore the message.

Given the improvement in our fight against illegal drugs,[1] how did cocaine and crack use become epidemic in only a few years? How did marijuana get to be one of the United States' largest cash crops?

Some people place the blame not on the drugs, but on the laws against them. They are saying we ought to take a second look at these laws. That, like alcohol prohibition, drug laws are futile. That, in fact, the laws may actually cause more problems than they solve. That they are more harmful than some of the drugs they prohibit.

If there were no drug laws, these people are telling us, there would never be the crimes associated with drugs; never the black market; never the billions of dollars illegally laundered; never the stealing, dealing, or murder over drugs; never the drug lords. And to replace all these problems, there would be over $10 billion in tax revenues a year to spend preventing and treating drug abuse.

If drug laws were liberalized, or even repealed, might drug use and drug addiction spiral upward to create a situation even more intolerable than what we already have? Maybe, like Sisyphus's struggle, the war on drugs is hopeless. Maybe, like Vietnam, this war is unwinnable. Maybe, it is time to let the rock roll down the mountain and turn our attention to other problems.

And maybe not. Yet it is worthwhile to take a look at what some people are saying about legalizing drugs.

Who are these people calling for change? Former hippies who want to legalize their marijuana plants and smoke a few joints? Discouraged prosecutors who believe that trying to bust the major drug cartels is like trying to hold back a tidal wave with a sandbag wall? Customs officers who know the impossibility of sealing off all U.S. borders? Neighbors who are tired of putting up with crack dealers in their communities? Civil libertarians who think what we do with our bodies is none of the government's business, who don't like the government snooping around our trash or spying over our property? Taxpayers weary of footing the bill for the war against drugs? Terminally ill cancer patients who want a shot of heroin to ease their pain? They are all of these.

Those who propose repealing drug laws are found everywhere. They are among our most conservative spokespersons. Milton Friedman, a conservative economist, believes that drug laws should be repealed. William F. Buckley, Jr., a conservative editor who initially opposed legalizing heroin, recently changed his mind. "Accumulated evidence draws me away from my own opposition," he wrote. "What we have now is a drug problem plus a crime problem plus a problem of a huge export of capital to the dope-producing countries."[2]

Drug law reformers are also found among our most liberal thinkers. Louis Nizer, an eminent legal scholar, suggests legalizing drugs, then making them available to addicts at a low cost through government-run clinics. "It would cost the government only 20 cents for a heroin shot," Nizer says, "compared to more than $100 addicts now pay."[3]

Many people connected to law enforcement, politics, and the justice system also support legalization. When they speak out for legalization, however, they risk public disapproval and perhaps even damage to their careers. So most remain silent on the issue.

One politician, though, did muster the courage to speak out. He is Kurt Schmoke, the mayor of Baltimore.

Before being elected as mayor, Schmoke was a federal prosecutor. On his job, he saw daily how difficult it was to win the war on drugs through the law. After his election, he decided it was time for a new approach. In April 1988, at the annual U.S. Conference of Mayors, Schmoke boldly suggested legalizing drugs. Then he called on Congress to hold hearings to debate the issue.

As chairman of the House Select Committee on Narcotics Abuse and Control, Representative Charles B. Rangel, a Democrat from New York, was responsible for any hearings on drugs. Rangel is an outspoken critic of legalizing drugs. At first, he rejected Schmoke's proposal to hold a hearing. "I strongly object to even the mention of legalization as an option,"[4] Rangel wrote. But shortly thereafter, in the heat of a television debate on Ted Koppel's "Nightline" program, Rangel agreed to chair a hearing.

During the two-day congressional hearing held a few weeks before the 1988 presidential election, more than thirty witnesses submitted testimony about legalization to the Select Narcotics Committee.

Experts both for and against legalization expressed their opinions. Some, like Ed Koch, then mayor of New York, were outraged at even having to discuss the issue. Said Koch in his speech to the committee, "I find it *astounding* that I am here to discuss a notion that seems to me to be the equivalent of extinguishing a fire with napalm."

Said another opponent, Dr. Charles R. Schuster, director of the National Institute on Drug Abuse (NIDA), "Legalization is not the answer . . . [solving the drug problem] is a long and difficult road, but we must not make it longer and harder by adding the potholes and pitfalls of legalization."

Others, like Arnold Trebach, founder of the Drug Policy Foundation, an educational organization dedicated to the issue of legalizing certain drugs, welcomed the opportunity to address Congress. Joining him were other noted scholars on drug policy, including John Kaplan, Ph.D., of Stanford, Ethan Nadelman, Ph.D., of Princeton, and Dr. David Musto and Dr. Lester Grinspoon of Harvard.

Banner headlines and cover stories on legalization followed. But soon the roar of legalization was reduced to a din in the tumult of the crack epidemic. The war on drugs continued.

In fact, a drug czar was appointed to head the attack against drugs. In his first report to Congress six months after assuming the role, William Bennett pronounced the idea of legalization a "national disaster."[5]

Despite the recent flurry of interest, legalization is neither a new nor a popular idea. Only a hundred years ago, all drugs were legal. In 1914, Congress first enacted federal drug laws,

16

with passage of the Harrison Act, a law restricting the non-medical use of narcotics. Ever since that time, advocates have pressed for repeal of drug laws.

Interest in drug law reform was renewed during the 1960s and 1970s, when drug use escalated. A few states went as far as decriminalizing the possession of small amounts of marijuana. For the most part, however, the laws have gotten more restrictive and the penalties for breaking them tougher.

POPULAR OPINION

According to a 1989 Gallup poll, drug abuse is the American public's leading concern.[6] Few Americans view legalization as a way out of the maze.

In a 1988 poll that ABC News conducted, 90 percent of respondents opposed legalizing all drugs, 51 percent believed drug use would increase under legalization, and 64 percent believed that organized crime would not be out of business if drugs were legalized.[7]

Other polls buttressed ABC's findings. In the 1989 Gallup poll mentioned above, nearly eight out of ten respondents favored tougher laws against drug users as a way to win the drug war. Nine out of ten believed tougher sanctions against drug dealing are necessary.[8]

Much of the opposition to legalization is based on the fear that if drugs were legalized, their use would increase, as well as all the problems associated with drugs—burnout, drug-related crime, impaired judgment at work, overdose, and death.

During the 1970s, the public was softer on the issue of legalization, particularly of marijuana. After a decade-long war on drugs, and growing evidence that marijuana is not harmless, even that issue finds little support.

In the same Gallup poll, respondents expressed the fear that the legalization of marijuana would send the wrong message: "Drugs are okay to use." It's a message few people, including drug reform advocates, want to give.

17

LOBBYING FOR CHANGE

In addition to individuals who support drug law reform, there are several groups and organizations advocating change. Since 1974, for example, the National Committee on the Treatment of Intractable Pain has lobbied Congress to make heroin available to terminally ill cancer patients.

Legalization is one of the issues embraced by the American Civil Liberties Union (ACLU), which challenges the constitutionality of drug laws. Of particular concern to the organization is the methods used to enforce drug laws— methods like wiretapping, paying informants, conducting searches without warrants, and random testing for drugs.

One of the organizations most dedicated to the issue is the National Organization for the Reform of Marijuana Laws (NORML). It was founded in 1970 to educate the public and the policymakers about marijuana and marijuana laws. NORML's primary focus is on legalizing marijuana, which it insists is only as good or bad as the people who use it.

NORML has filed several lawsuits over the years. One suit led the way to the development of the first synthetic THC pill (the active ingredient in marijuana), which allows chemotherapy patients to legally use the drug. Another suit was against the federal government for spraying illegally grown marijuana crops with the herbicide paraquat.

In 1986, the Oregon Marijuana Initiative (OMI) collected enough signatures to get a proposition for marijuana legalization on the state ballot. Only 27 percent of the voters supported the proposition. Had it been approved, homegrown marijuana would have been legalized. Despite the defeat, according to the chief petitioner, Laird Funk, OMI intends to keep on trying.[9]

Drug reform is a topic studied by several "think tanks," organizations that employ scholars to research issues and share their findings. Two major think tanks exploring drug policy are the Cato Institute and the Rand Corporation.

One think tank, the Drug Policy Foundation, is devoted

exclusively to the issue of drug law reform. Founded in 1986 by Arnold Trebach, an American University professor, the Drug Policy Foundation regularly holds forums on Capitol Hill to inform politicians about the issue. In addition, the foundation sponsors an annual conference at which scholars convene to share research and ideas.

A newcomer to the legalization issue is the International Anti-Prohibition League on Drugs. It was begun by Italy's Radical Party, which hosted a three-day congress in April 1989. Lawyers, doctors, scholars, and police officers from twelve Western nations gathered in Rome to discuss the possibility of worldwide legalization of drugs.

"The crime that results [from drug prohibition]," said one of the league's spokespersons, "endangers ordinary citizens and threatens the stability of states . . . the modern version of [alcohol] prohibition has turned great cities into battlefields."[10]

Judging by the polls, the American public has not been swayed by the arguments for legalization.

And despite the candor of politicians like Mayor Schmoke or the persuasion of groups like NORML, neither has Congress. Ironically, many liberal politicians use the drug war as a chance to show conservative voters how "tough" they can be on an issue. Moreover, as long as public opinion is so staunchly against illegal drug use, even officials who privately support drug law reform will not publicly do so. This is especially true for police officers, whose job it is to uphold laws, not to criticize them.

Our courts are also unlikely sites for legalization. They continue to uphold drug testing and broaden the definition of search and seizure. The Supreme Court even upheld a ban on selling drug paraphernalia or running "head shops."

Thus, until a groundswell of support or a radical change of thinking develops, legalization is unlikely to occur. Meanwhile, it remains an alternative to explore, albeit an unpopular one.

2

HISTORY OF REGULATION

If we fight this war as a divided nation, then the war is lost. But if we face this evil as a nation united, this will be nothing but a handful of useless chemicals.
—President George Bush

Before the discovery of modern drugs, doctors could cure few diseases and had only a small number of drugs to treat the symptoms from which their patients suffered.

Nineteenth-century doctors relied on the drugs that were available, chiefly quinine, opium, and morphine (a derivative of opium). Because opiates were effective for a wide range of symptoms, they were considered to be indispensable. They were used for pain, sleeplessness, diarrhea, anxiety, even insanity. In addition, opiates were prescribed for diseases that were common then, such as malaria, smallpox, syphilis, and tuberculosis. Besides relieving so many physical symptoms, opiates relaxed patients, giving them a pleasurable, euphoric feeling.

So essential was opium in medicine, that in 1778, Dr. Thaddeus Betts advised: "Opium is an article which no physician is ought ever to want; it is so extensively useful, and in cases so perilous and urgent, where no substitute will supply its defect, that physicians . . . would be lame and deficient

20

without it.''[1] Dr. Betts ensured his own supply of opium by growing and harvesting poppies, a practice he recommended to his colleagues.

In 1856 European doctors introduced their American colleagues to the hypodermic syringe. Because the hypodermic injects drugs directly into a muscle or vein, it is stronger and quicker than taking it orally. At first, American doctors were skeptical. By 1881, however, their skepticism had turned to enthusiasm.

David T. Courtwright, a historian and an expert on nineteenth-century addiction, observed: "A syringe of morphine, in a very real sense, was a magic wand. It could cure little, but it could relieve anything . . . doctors and patients alike were tempted to overuse it."[2]

Taking opiates, even for the duration of one illness, can result in addiction, sometimes for life. Such addiction is called iatrogenic, which means "doctor-caused."

During the late 1800s, opium and morphine were prescribed so often that there was an alarming amount of iatrogenic addiction. No doubt several epidemics—two cholera and one dysentery—contributed to addiction rates. So, too, did the Civil War.

During the Civil War, thousands of soldiers became addicted following narcotic treatment for their battle wounds and illnesses. In the war's aftermath, so many soldiers were addicted—between 45,000 and 50,000—that drug addiction became known as the "soldier's disease."

According to Courtwright, the typical opium or morphine addict was a middle- or upper-class housewife, who first became addicted between the ages of twenty-five and forty-five after being treated with a narcotic for a medical problem. More addicts were found in the South than anywhere else, probably because diseases like malaria, typhoid, cholera, and dysentery were most prevalent there.

Doctors, dentists, and pharmacists had easy access to narcotics. They also tended to treat themselves. Not surprisingly, then, their rates of addiction were quite high.

Poor people could rarely afford a physician's care. As a

21

result, they were spared doctors' attention, the prescriptions for narcotics, and, consequently, much doctor-caused addiction. Instead of a doctor's care, however, poor people resorted to home remedies and "patent medicines" that were cheaper.

These patent medicines were concoctions sold through the mail, over the counter, and by door-to-door salesmen. Their manufacturers and distributors made wild claims about their products' effectiveness. They also kept the ingredients a secret, particularly the addictive ones like opium, morphine, heroin, and cocaine. Because the ingredients were concealed, many consumers unwittingly got hooked on the patent medicines without knowing why.

This type of drug use was widespread. Some mothers gave their babies "soothing formulas" laced with opium and heroin. Women took palliatives with narcotics to ease menstrual cramps. Other people consumed the likes of Ayer's Cherry Pectoral, Mrs. Winslow's Soothing Syrup, and Dover's Powder, all of which contained addictive drugs.

Ironically, some addicts resorted to patent medicines to help cure their addiction. Unfortunately, they were simply trading one addiction for another.

It is possible that too much blame has been placed on patent medicines as a cause of long-term addiction. Since users were unaware of the narcotics in the medicines, when they withdrew from them, they may have mistaken withdrawal symptoms for a new illness. Furthermore, babies weaned from soothing medicines probably suffered withdrawal symptoms that their mothers mistakenly attributed to other causes.[3] Regardless, patent medicines must have contributed to short-term, if not to long-term, addiction.

After 1870, narcotics were so widely prescribed and used that addiction was also widespread. So widespread, in fact, that the end of the century became known as a "dope fiend's paradise."[4]

By the turn of the century, however, a great deal had been learned about the origins of disease and illness. "Germ theory" gained acceptance, and with it came new discoveries in treating illnesses.

22

Vaccinations against typhoid fever, drugs to treat syphilis, and increased knowledge about bacteria and the spread of diseases such as dysentery and other digestive disorders eliminated much of the medical need for narcotics. New drugs like aspirin, novocaine, and anti-inflammatories replaced narcotics and cocaine. Consequently, opium, morphine, and heroin were increasingly overlooked in favor of the more effective, less addictive alternatives.

Thus, by 1910, new cases of doctor-caused or patent medicine addiction were not so common. Still, there remained an alarming number of addicts. The addicts usually kept their addiction a secret. They were mostly docile, harmless people, and so the public showed little concern for them. To the medical community, however, they were a grave concern.

NONMEDICAL ADDICTION

Americans were exposed to addictive drugs. Laudanum, a popular opium-laced preparation, had been used since the Pilgrims arrived in America. Coca-Cola's original secret formula, created in 1886 by John Styth Pemberton, was advertised as a nonalcoholic "temperance" drink. Before the company switched to caffeine in 1903, a glass of Coke originally contained a significant amount of cocaine.[5]

During the second half of the nineteenth century, drugs became popular for reasons that had nothing to do with medicine. With this recreational use came addiction.

A widespread recreational use of drugs was opium smoking. Introduced in the U.S. by Chinese immigrants, opium smoking gained acceptance among gamblers, thieves, and prostitutes. There were also a few smokers among the upper class and avant-garde. For the most part, though, opium was smoked in special rooms called opium dens and primarily confined to the Chinese and society's outcasts.

Another addictive drug that gained popularity was cocaine, known for its ability to enhance strength and endurance. Wrote one stevedore about cocaine: "I can work up to seventy hours at a stretch without sleep or rest, in rain, in cold and in heat."[6]

23

Marijuana was introduced by Mexican immigrants around 1910. It soon grew popular among Southern blacks and certain musicians and artists. (Only later, during the Vietnam War years, did marijuana become popular among soldiers, students, and eventually the mainstream.)

Heroin was first marketed in 1898 by a German pharmaceutical firm, the Bayer Company (which also held the patent on aspirin). Like morphine, heroin was touted as a miracle drug with no side effects. Its medical use was mainly to treat respiratory ailments (effective, no doubt, because it relaxed sufferers). Soon, however, heroin's potential for addiction became well known. It, too, became part of an underground drug culture.

It is difficult to be accurate about the number of addicts in America at the turn of the century. By then, new iatrogenic addiction was rare, but other addiction was not. Experts estimate that addiction to opium reached its peak at that time, and that altogether in the United States, there were probably between 200,000 and 400,000 addicts.[7]

PRESSURE TO BAN DRUGS

In 1875, San Francisco became the first of several municipalities to ban opium smoking and to close opium dens. Cities and states with large Chinese populations, where opium was popular, followed suit.

By the 1900s, there was mounting pressure at the federal level to do something about the opium problem. Congress passed a law in 1909 that prohibited the sale of opium. Since the law was aimed at groups like Chinese immigrants, gamblers, and prostitutes—those detested by the American public—there was little protest over it.

There was also mounting concern about the dangerous drugs in patent medicines and drinks like laudanum and Coke. In response, Congress passed the first Pure Food and Drug Act in 1906. This new law required that all active ingredients be noted on a product's label. The public veil of ignorance was lifted. Though it did nothing to help those already addicted, the law did curb new addiction and discouraged manufacturers from using addictive drugs in their products.

THE HAGUE CONVENTION

China had a major opium addiction problem among its citizens. It sought to bar imports of opium, chiefly from Britain, which had damaged Chinese society and drained wealth overseas. Britain, seeking to end trade restrictions imposed by China, used this as an opportunity for war. In the first Opium War (1839–42), Britain forced China to expand trade and to cede Hong Kong. A second war (1856–58) opened more Chinese ports.

With the loss to Britain, addiction in China increased. By the end of the century, there were nearly ninety million opium addicts in the country.

In 1909, the United States wanted to open trading with China's huge market. The U.S. also had inherited a narcotics problem in the Philippines. As a goodwill gesture to China and as a way to solve the Philippine drug problem, it proposed international control of the narcotics trade.

A conference was held in Shanghai, China, in 1909 to discuss such control. Two years later, a second conference was held in The Hague, Netherlands.

At the second conference, an accord was reached. The treaty, the Hague Convention of 1912, was signed by thirty-four participating nations, which agreed to control narcotics. Among their decisions was that the use of opium be limited to the practice of medicine. Other uses, such as recreational smoking, were strongly condemned.

To control the narcotics trade, each nation agreed to set a quota on how much it would import or export, a quota limited to medical purposes.

Despite success in negotiating the treaty, the United States found itself in an embarrassing situation. It had been the U.S.'s idea to impose international control of narcotics. Yet on its own soil, there was little control. Indeed, opium imports were legal and had raised nearly $27 million in tax revenues.

THE HARRISON ACT

In order to rectify this situation, U.S. delegates to the Hague Convention convinced Congress to pass a law restricting opium and cocaine. Thus, on December 17, 1914, the Harrison Act became law. It went into effect a few months later.

The new law allowed opium and cocaine to be sold in small quantities over the counter. More important, larger amounts could be prescribed by doctors or dentists. Their only restrictions were to record the transactions and register themselves with a central agency. Those who manufactured or dispensed drugs were also subject to the same regulations.

Withdrawal from addictive drugs is unpleasant, and sometimes dangerous. An addict may experience convulsions, cramps, nausea, chills, sweating, and depression. Sudden withdrawal can even cause an addict to die.

Besides the physical symptoms, addicts often experience psychological ones. Even if they stay off drugs for months, even years, they may continue to crave the drug's effect. This craving can be as difficult to overcome and as debilitating as any physical dependency.

There has always been debate over why people get addicted to drugs and how to overcome the addiction. One theory is that chemically dependent people have a medical problem, that perhaps they have inherited a tendency to use and abuse drugs. A more popular theory is that drug use and abuse is really a social issue, a moral weakness.

Regardless of the reasons for addiction, there has never been treatment that is 100 percent successful, nor is every addict willing to undergo treatment.

When the Harrison Act went into effect, many physicians continued to prescribe drugs to patients who were addicts. Pharmacists also continued selling prescriptions. Some physicians and pharmacists did so out of genuine concern and compassion for those addicted to drugs.

Other physicians, known as "dope doctors," cashed in on the new law. They prescribed drugs to anyone who wanted them, sometimes filling hundreds of prescriptions a day. (There were unscrupulous pharmacists as well.) Many of these prescriptions were to opium smokers and other recreational users who could no longer obtain a legal drug supply. Other nonmedical users turned to the mushrooming black market, while still others turned to crime to pay the exorbitant prices illegal drugs now commanded.

Originally, the Harrison Act was meant only to regulate the sale of narcotics. It was not intended to ban them altogether. However, the legislation ultimately banned all but medical drug use, an outcome that no doubt surprised a number of its original supporters.

How did a law meant to regulate drugs wind up prohibiting them?

With the end of World War I, there was fear that drug use would limit the nation's ability to defend itself militarily in case of another war. There was also a strong movement against alcohol consumption, which culminated in the passage of the Eighteenth Amendment in 1919. Added to this was the popular notion that drug use was a sign of moral weakness. Together these concerns caused the Harrison Act to be reinterpreted.

In 1919, the issue was put to the Supreme Court in the case of *Webb, et al.* v. *United States.* Based on a single clause in the Harrison Act—that drugs could be legally dispensed only in the course of professional practice[8]—the court decided that professional practice excluded giving drugs to people just to maintain their drug habits. "It is so plain a perversion of meaning," the justices explained in their decision, "that no discussion of the subject is required."[9]

Reinterpretation of the Harrison Act denied addicts any legal source of drugs. In addition, physicians and pharmacists who continued to supply them were subject to arrest. Indeed, after the *Webb, et al.* decision, hundreds of physicians and pharmacists were arrested.

In 1925, the Court declared addiction to be a medical, not a criminal, matter, a position reaffirmed in 1962. But while it was not a crime to be an addict, it was (and still is) illegal for an addict or anyone else to use illicit drugs.

Since the Harrison Act, many new drug laws have been enacted. The first was in 1924, when the Harrison Act was amended to prohibit heroin. In 1937 the Marijuana Tax Act was passed, restricting marijuana use. By 1970, a total of fifty-five federal laws had been passed restricting or prohibiting drug use.

THE WAR ON DRUGS

During the 1960s, illicit drug use increased dramatically. At least half the U.S. soldiers who served in Vietnam used drugs. When they returned, a fifth were chemically dependent. Although most managed to get off drugs, the situation so alarmed the U.S. military that they became the first to initiate drug testing.

Another concern was the alarming increase in drug use among the nation's youth. By 1969, 24 million Americans over age eleven had used marijuana at least once. In addition, 188,000 had been arrested for possessing it, a tenfold increase in just five years.

In response to the crisis, in June 1971, President Richard M. Nixon declared war on drugs.

One of the first steps the federal government took was to consolidate the fifty-five drug laws into a uniform law known as the Controlled Substance Act (CSA). Another was to establish the Commission on Marijuana and Drug Abuse, whose task it was to report to Congress and make recommendations.

After two years, the commission presented its report with several recommendations. Although composed of many conservative members, the commission suggested that marijuana be decriminalized. This meant that users would be fined, rather than arrested, for possession of small amounts of marijuana. Since there were many agencies responsible for drug enforcement and treatment programs, the commission also recommended forming a single federal agency to oversee all federal drug efforts. Finally, the commission stressed that the problems of alcohol and tobacco, which are legal drugs, should not be overlooked.

Less than three years after he had declared war on drugs, Nixon announced that the nation had turned a corner. Despite his optimism, he ignored the commission's recommendation to decriminalize marijuana.

The next two administrations embraced a more tolerant drug policy. President Jimmy Carter boldly suggested adopting the commission's recommendation to decriminalize marijuana. Between 1973 and 1979, this is precisely what eleven states—Oregon, Alaska, Maine, Colorado, California, Ohio, Minnesota, Mississippi, North Carolina, New York, and Nebraska—did.

Soon, however, the issue of drug use emerged again as a paramount national concern. Some of this was due to the media's attention to the drug tragedies of several famous people. These included the drug overdose deaths of Len Bias, a budding basketball star, and John Belushi, a well-known comedian. Richard Pryor also received attention when he suffered serious burns from an accident that occurred while he freebased cocaine.

During his second term in office, President Ronald Reagan declared a second war on drugs. To fight this new war, he urged Congress to pass the Omnibus Drug Bill, which went into effect in 1984. The bill allocated a record amount of money to the drug war chest and established more stringent sentencing of drug felons.

By 1987, overall drug use had decreased. But the crack epidemic and its searing effect on crime, health, even Latin American politics, scared the American public into demands

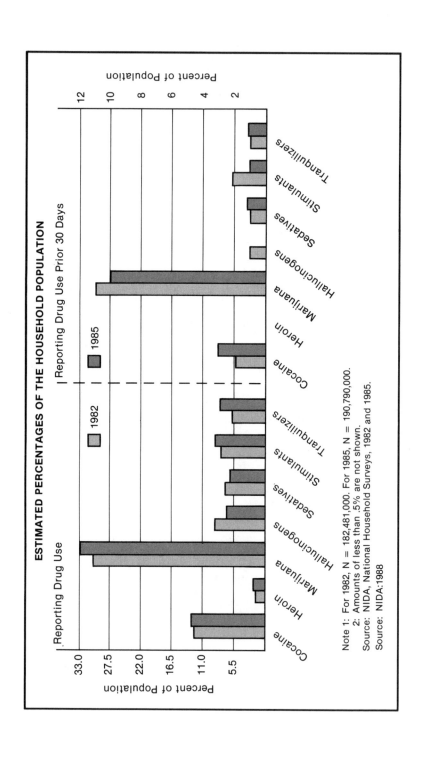

ESTIMATED PERCENTAGES OF THE HOUSEHOLD POPULATION

| Reporting Drug Use | Reporting Drug Use Prior 30 Days

■ 1982   ■ 1985

Percent of Population

33.0 27.5 22.0 16.5 11.0 5.5

Cocaine, Heroin, Marijuana, Hallucinogens, Sedatives, Stimulants, Tranquilizers

Cocaine, Heroin, Marijuana, Hallucinogens, Sedatives, Stimulants, Tranquilizers

Percent of Population

12 10 8 6 4 2

Note 1: For 1982, N = 182,481,000. For 1985, N = 190,790,000.
    2: Amounts of less than .5% are not shown.
Source: NIDA, National Household Surveys, 1982 and 1985.
Source: NIDA:1988

that more stringent measures be taken to win the war on drugs. In addition, the threat of AIDS among intravenous drug users had escalated.

Thus, in 1989, newly elected President George Bush appointed William Bennett to lead the nation's war on drugs, dubbing him the ''drug czar.''

In his first report to Congress after six months of research, Bennett suggested that the U.S. could win the war on drugs only by stepping up its efforts, including spending. Bennett was optimistic that over the next ten years, drug use could be cut in half. Which, of course, still leaves America with the problem of what to do with the other half.

Mind-altering drugs have been used for centuries, and for centuries their use was legal. It is the laws restricting drugs that are newcomers, less than a century old.

The history of U.S. drug laws is closely tied to a growing concern about and knowledge of the harmful effects of certain drugs. As the medical community replaced addictive drugs with safer, more effective ones, the government grew intolerant of recreational drug use. Today's laws reflect this intolerance and the concern about the medical, psychological, and social effects of drugs. They also reflect the opinion that drug use is a moral, not a medical, issue. Finally, they reflect a historic concern to protect Americans from unsafe drug use.

Years before the federal government publicly waged a war on drugs, the battle began with passage of the first drug laws. More laws and more battles followed. At the heart of the war is whether these laws can be enforced and whether, indeed, they cause more harm than the drugs themselves.

3

LAWS AGAINST DRUGS

Drugs are not bad because they're illegal.
They're illegal because they're bad.
—*John Lawn, head of the Drug*
Enforcement Agency (DEA)

There are thousands of drugs. Though a few have been around since antiquity, most have been discovered only recently, particularly during the last two decades. Some, like insulin, antibiotics, aspirin, and novocaine, ushered in a remarkable era of health and longevity. Never in medical history have so many symptoms, illnesses, and diseases been so treatable or so curable.

Some drugs are natural, taken mostly from herbs or other plants. Opium is extracted from the juice of unripe seedpods of the opium poppy (*Papavera somniferum*), while nicotine, cocaine, marijuana, and hashish all come from the leaves of plants. Effects of these drugs have been known for hundreds, perhaps even thousands, of years, and they have been used for medical, religious, and recreational purposes.

Other drugs come from natural sources that are chemically processed. Alcohol, for example, is distilled or refined from grains or fruits, while morphine and heroin are isolated chemically from opium.

Today, the majority of drugs are manmade, or synthetic. Sometimes they are identical to drugs found naturally, but more often they are completely new chemical compounds. Examples of synthetic drugs include Valium, LSD, PCP, amphetamines, and aspirin.

REGULATING DRUGS

Not all drugs are banned. Indeed, alcohol, tobacco, and caffeine are quite legal. Moreover, just because a drug is legal does not mean that the government believes it is safe. Former Surgeon General C. Everett Koop repeatedly warned the public that some legal drugs are also some of our most harmful. For each year, almost 650,000 people die due to the effects of alcohol or tobacco. In addition, alcohol contributes to a third of all highway deaths and a half million highway injuries, and is associated with half of all violent crimes.[1]

Although legal drugs are not prohibited, they are regulated. For example, cigarettes may not be sold to minors nor smoked in certain places such as planes. Through warning labels, media spots, and programs like National Smokeout Days, the public is educated about the harm of smoking, in the hopes of reducing the demand for cigarettes.

As it does for dangerous legal drugs, the government wages educational campaigns and offers treatment programs to reduce the demand for illicit drugs.

In a federal study reported by the National Institute on Drug Abuse, the number of people who said they had used an illegal drug during one year was 25 percent less than the number who had used one the previous year.[2] Still, though the number of casual users has declined, the number of people addicted to cocaine has increased, and overall drug use remains high. Moreover, Americans now consume over half the world's supply of illegal drugs, a trend that shows little signs of diminishing.[3]

TRIED AN ILLICIT DRUG IN LIFETIME
72,000,000

USED DRUGS WITHIN THE YEAR
27,000,000

ABUSE DRUGS: ADDICTS–
1,100,000 to 2,000,000

Source: NIDA:1988

CONTROLLED SUBSTANCE ACT

As we learned in the previous chapter, the foundation for all current drug laws is the Controlled Substance Act (CSA). Since its passage in 1970, the CSA's provisions have been strengthened, most recently with passage of the 1986 Omnibus Drug Act.

The CSA regulates the manufacture and distribution of dangerous drugs: narcotics, cannabis, stimulants, amphetamines, and hallucinogens. As a federal law, it is the "law of the land." This means that states and counties may impose stricter regulations and penalties for violations—and some do—but they must adhere to, at the very least, the CSA's minimum guidelines.

The purpose of the CSA is to ensure that dangerous drugs be used only for medical purposes, and that when they are used, they be used safely. Not all prescription drugs are regulated by the CSA. In fact, most are not.

The CSA has defined five categories, or "schedules," as they are called, for the drugs it does regulate. Any drug that is addictive or has the potential to be abused is regulated by the CSA and placed in one of the five schedules.

Schedule I is the most restrictive; drugs in this category are banned or allowed only for strictly supervised medical experimentation. Schedule II drugs are also highly restricted.

Schedule III, IV, and V drugs are monitored and regulated, but they seldom require a physician's prescription; many are sold over the counter.

A drug's schedule can change if new information suggests that it is either more or less dangerous than was previously believed. For example, amphetamines used to be sold over the counter. But as amphetamine abuse became widespread, they were rescheduled to a stricter category.

Three criteria are used to judge each drug and determine if it should be scheduled at all, and if so, in which schedule it should be placed. These criteria are how the drug is used in

35

medicine, how it can be potentially abused, and how safe it is to use.

Medical Use

Very few drugs are totally illegal. Rather, it is their use that determines their legal status. Take morphine. Administered by a physician to a patient who has just undergone surgery, morphine is legal. But injected into the veins of a junkie, it is not.

Dangerous drugs are not supposed to be used to have a good time, to relax, stay awake, or perform better. Instead, they are supposed to be for medical purposes—to help people feel better and to improve their health.

Because most hallucinogens have no recognized medical use, they are categorized as Schedule I, highly restricted drugs. Heroin is also a Schedule I drug, not because it has no medical use, but because its use is now considered obsolete. Not all physicians or patients agree on the medical utility of heroin. In fact, it is still used to relieve pain in hospice programs treating terminally ill patients in England.

A major issue in the legalization debate is whether a drug has to have a recognized medical use. After all, argue proponents of legalization, drugs like alcohol and tobacco do not have medical uses. Drawing on that analogy, they claim that marijuana, for example, which is a Schedule I drug and available only for authorized medical experimentation, ought to be completely unscheduled.

Potential for Abuse

According to the U.S. Department of Justice, which regulates the CSA, the threshold issue for regulating dangerous drugs is their "potential for abuse." If none exists, a drug cannot be controlled.

Potential for abuse refers to how people tend to use a drug. Do many people use it without a doctor's prescription? Anabolic steroids require a prescription but are increasingly being sold illegally without one. Because of such widespread abuse outside the medical field, it is possible, and perhaps likely,

36

that anabolic steroids will become a scheduled drug. Moreover, scheduling them would increase the penalties for those who are caught misusing them.

Another question asked of a drug is this: When it is used, does the drug threaten the user's safety or that of others?

Cynthia Harris founded STOP! The Madness Foundation to fight drugs and crime after her son, Lionel, was murdered in a parking lot. His killer was free, pending a trial for another crime. When arrested, he tested positive for PCP, a mood-altering drug that makes some users paranoid or violent, the reason PCP is so strictly scheduled.

Still another concern is whether a drug is being used by a lot of people who don't need it. Is it trendy or ''in'' to be using it? Like anabolic steroids or crack, is a drug suddenly more popular than ever? Is there danger of its widespread use? People took LSD and Quaaludes to have a novel experience, to get high or to mellow out, or because it was the thing to do. Dangerous drugs whose use becomes widespread and largely nonmedical are likely to be reevaluated and tightly scheduled.

Safety Or Dependence
Liability
A drug's safety is an important criterion. Unsafe, unpredictable drugs are strictly scheduled. It must be determined whether a drug will cause dangerously high blood pressure, hallucinations, bizarre behavior, or other unsafe effects, even under medical supervision.

Dependence liability is another factor in judging a drug's liability. What are the chances that users will become dependent on a drug? How much can they take before they become addicted and suffer withdrawal symptoms if they stop taking the drug? Drugs like crack and heroin, which are highly addictive, are tightly scheduled.

A drug is physically addictive if users suffer physical symptoms—nausea, chills, even death—when they stop taking it. Certain drugs, such as cocaine and amphetamines, are harmful because they cause users to become psychologically dependent on them. Addicts will crave the drug and believe they have to have it, even though they suffer from few or no physical symptoms.

REGULATION

The Controlled Substance Act regulates the manufacture and distribution of all scheduled drugs. Anyone handling these drugs must be registered with the Drug Enforcement Agency, a federal agency in the Justice Department. It is illegal to purchase scheduled drugs from anyone not registered with the DEA.

Records of sales and inventory must be kept for scheduled drugs. These records help drug enforcement people find out who is excessively selling, prescribing, or buying scheduled drugs, and perhaps abusing them. For drugs on the less restricted schedules, the record may be as simple as keeping a list of purchasers' signatures.

Quotas are set for the amount of Schedule I and II drugs that may be manufactured in the United States each year.

Finally, the CSA sets minimum standards for storing scheduled drugs. In some states, Schedule I and II drugs must be stored in vaults or burglar-proof safes, while other drugs that are classified in a restricted schedule need only be kept off-limits to the public (such as behind the counter where the pharmacist dispenses prescriptions).

WHO BREAKS THE
DRUG LAWS?

Every time a scheduled drug is not used according to the CSA's guidelines, a law is broken. Every time a scheduled drug is grown, processed, manufactured, sold, or bought by someone not registered with the DEA, a law is broken. Every time someone merely possesses an illicit drug in his or her house, car, boat, or barn, a law is broken. And those laws are broken by millions of citizens every day.

Periodically, the National Institute on Drug Abuse (NIDA), a federal agency supervising research on drugs, conducts a survey of drug use in the United States called the National Household Survey. According to the most recent survey results, more than 72 million people—more than one out of every three Americans—have tried an illicit drug at least once in their lifetime. Twenty-three million use illicit drugs at least once a month. In 1988, a million people tried cocaine for the first time, while nearly half a million were addicted to it.[4]

Abbie Hoffman, a famous activist from the sixties, broke the law when he sold a few ounces of cocaine. His "buyer" was an undercover narcotics agent, who promptly arrested Hoffman. Before his trial, Hoffman skipped bail and escaped to Canada, where he assumed a new identity. Later, still avoiding the law with a false identity, he snuck back into the U.S.

Hoffman gave up not only his identity to avoid arrest but also any contact with his friends and family. This meant he could not sit at his dying father's bedside or attend his father's funeral. Nor could he participate in his son's birthday parties or watch him play sports.

After years of living "underground," Hoffman turned himself over to federal agents. He served a federal prison sentence before finally returning to public life. In 1989, Hoffman committed suicide with a drug overdose.

Hoffman's story is unique. But his violations are not.

WHO ENFORCES THE LAW?

Drug laws are enforced by all levels of government: local, county, state, and federal. Where drugs are an especially critical problem, such as in Miami, Florida, special task forces have been created to combine the efforts of the different law enforcement agencies.

In 1973, to streamline efforts, President Nixon merged the five federal anti-drug agencies into a single Justice Department agency, the Drug Enforcement Agency, or DEA, as it is commonly known. The DEA works closely with other federal

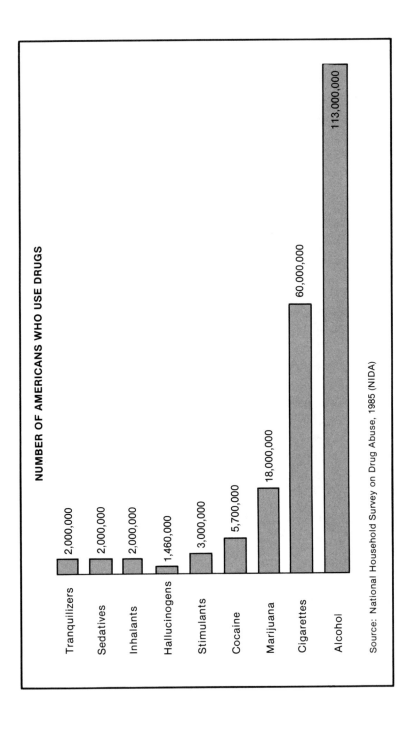

NUMBER OF AMERICANS WHO USE DRUGS

Tranquilizers — 2,000,000

Sedatives — 2,000,000

Inhalants — 2,000,000

Hallucinogens — 1,460,000

Stimulants — 3,000,000

Cocaine — 5,700,000

Marijuana — 18,000,000

Cigarettes — 60,000,000

Alcohol — 113,000,000

Source: National Household Survey on Drug Abuse, 1985 (NIDA)

agencies like U.S. Customs, the FBI, the State Department, and the U.S. Coast Guard, as well as local and foreign agencies in need of advice or assistance.

In 1988, federal agents seized 2,150 pounds of heroin, 198,000 pounds of cocaine, and 1,660,000 pounds of marijuana.[5] The previous year they had seized $655 million in assets—homes, cars, boats, stocks, bonds, bank accounts, and cash of suspects—that were an important part of illegal drug trading. As Joseph Keefe, a spokesman for the DEA, noted, "Six hundred fifty-five million dollars is well in excess of the agency's budget."[6]

To coordinate the entire federal drug strategy, a new agency was created called the National Drug Control Policy. Its director, known as the "drug czar," is responsible for providing a national strategy for implementing the Controlled Substance Act and for overcoming the nation's drug problem.

PENALTIES FOR BREAKING THE LAW

The 1986 Anti-Abuse Bill provided minimum penalties for breaking the federal drug laws. Its fines and sentences, particularly for repeat offenders, were stiffer than ever.

Though it does not require it, the CSA permits the death penalty for certain drug felonies. Speaking to an audience of Drug Enforcement Agency agents about the murder of one of the agents, President Bush vowed to press for mandatory death sentences for drug felons who murdered agents.

"Drug dealers need to understand a simple fact," he said. "You shoot a cop, and you will be severely punished, fast. And if I had my way, I'd say with your life."[7]

*   *   *

In their lifetime, many Americans have tried illicit drugs. Millions use them regularly. Most of these users are not dependent on drugs, but almost two million are. For them, life is a constant struggle to maintain their habit.

41

Given such widespread illicit drug use, the Controlled Substance Act clearly has not solved this problem. Perhaps, though, it has contained it, keeping more people from using as well as abusing drugs.

The federal government's goal is "zero tolerance," that is, no illicit drug use tolerance. That may be an elusive goal, as William Bennett, director of the National Drug Control Policy, has suggested. After all, laws against murder, rape, and child abuse have not stopped those crimes.

Laws are a society's prescription for a good and decent life. Laws are supposed to protect society's members from harming each other, and to punish those who do.

The question most drug law reformers ask is not whether drugs are as harmful as the CSA believes they are, for most agree that drugs like heroin, crack, and PCP are very dangerous. Instead, they pose the question President Jimmy Carter asked during his term in office: "Do drug laws do more harm than the drugs themselves do?"[8]

4

HOW WOULD LEGALIZATION WORK?

We need to clarify once and for all what we mean when we say legalization.

Would there be twenty-four-hour dispensaries for those who need a fix immediately? If you're not an addict, could you buy these drugs? If you are an addict, do you get to buy more than the person who is just "experimenting"? Will we have "drug stamps" for those who are jobless and want to satisfy their craving?

Can you take a "coke break" during lunch on the job? Can drugs be advertised on radio, TV, billboards at the ballparks and alongside city buses?

—*Representative Charles B. Rangel, chairman of the House Select Committee on Narcotics Abuse and Control*

Many questions are raised by legalization. Which drugs will be legal and which will not? Who will be able to purchase them—only registered addicts or anyone who wants to try them? Where will they be sold? Through government-run clinics? Or drugstores, liquor stores, and street vendors? How will the quality be controlled? Will a demand for more potent drugs create another black market? Who will set the prices? If they are too low, will too many people buy them? If they are too high, will people look for cheaper sources?

In 1988, the editors of *Reason* magazine asked some of the most outspoken supporters of drug legalization to describe how it would work.[1] The following are some of their answers:

David Boaz, *Vice-President of the Cato Institute*

Marijuana, cocaine, and heroin would be sold only in specially licensed stores—perhaps in liquor stores, perhaps in a new kind of drugstore. Warning labels would be posted in the stores and on the packages. It would be illegal to sell drugs to minors . . . to advertise drugs on television and possibly even in print. Committing a crime or driving under the influence of drugs would be illegal, as with alcohol.

Milton Friedman, *Nobel Prize Laureate in Economics*

Legalize all drugs. They could be sold through ordinary retail outlets . . . probably drugstores. There should be no FDA [Food and Drug Administration] or other controls on drugs. I shudder at the thought of a TV ad with a pretty woman saying, "My brand will give you a high such as you've never experienced." On the other hand, I have always been hesitant about restrictions on freedom of advertising for general free-speech reasons. I have little doubt that legalization would be impossible without substantial restrictions on advertising.

Georgette Bennett, *New York City Police Department advisor*

*Drug sales will be permitted only by government-
licensed vendors. Vendors will be restricted to
pharmacies and clinics. All decriminalized drug
products will be sold generically. Brand name
competition will be prohibited. The government
will distribute drug products to vendors, eliminating the commercial middleperson. The State
Department will negotiate directly with foreign
governments to import drugs. Strict price controls will keep prices low. For impoverished
adults, free drugs will be provided at government
clinics. Submission to treatment and rehabilitation programs will be mandatory. All commercial
advertising of drugs will be banned. Minimum-
age requirements will be established. Drug use
will be prohibited on and off duty at work. [There
will be] criminal sanctions for driving while
drug-impaired, circumventing regulations for legal sales of drugs, price gouging, selling through
unauthorized outlets, including mail or wire.*

CHANGING THE LAW

There are three major ways for drug law reform to occur: by
a court decision, a statute (a law enacted by the legislative
branch), or popular vote. All have been tried. Most have been
unsuccessful.

The Supreme Court is unlikely to repeal drug laws; at
least, not if their record on drug cases is considered. The court
has upheld random drug testing, searches without warrants,
and laws forbidding the sale of drug paraphernalia.

The public ballot is another unlikely source for drug reform. Referendums like Oregon's Marijuana Initiative find

their way to the ballots. But once there, they have repeatedly failed to acquire enough votes.

If reform does occur, according to David Boaz, a researcher from the Cato Institute, it will happen where laws are enacted—in the legislature—where prohibition also has its strongest roots.

DRUG REFORM OPTIONS

There are many ways to reform drug laws. The chief methods are repeal, legalization, de facto legalization, and decriminalization. Interestingly, not all of these reforms require changes in the law.

Repeal

At one extreme is repeal of all laws restricting or prohibiting drug use. In essence, repeal would be a return to pre–Harrison Act days, when there were no laws against drug use.

Libertarians support repeal. They believe that drug use is a private matter and the right of every adult citizen, a right that needs protection, not regulation. Consequently, libertarians do not want any drug laws. Instead they want to repeal at least certain of the drug laws.

In a letter to a *New York Times* editor, one writer explained the difference between repeal and legalization: "We are, after all, a democracy, and in a democracy we do not legalize things. For good reasons, we occasionally make things illegal, as we have in this case. . . . But we change our minds and repeal certain prohibitions."[2]

Legalization

Another approach would be to legalize certain drugs. Then their production and sale could be regulated by local, state, or federal bureaucrats.

Great Britain has already experimented with legalization. In 1924, the British Minister of Health asked leading physicians for advice on treating morphine and heroin addiction.

Two years later, the advice was delivered by the Rolleston Committee. In its report, the committee advised legalizing drugs for anyone who could not withdraw from them. This included people whose addictions required only small amounts of drugs and who, with long-term access to these small amounts, could live somewhat normal, useful lives.

Over the next forty years, British drug policy reflected the Rolleston Committee's advice. Physicians were permitted to prescribe controlled drugs to patients with long-term addictions. They could also prescribe heroin to terminally ill patients.

By most accounts, the British system worked well. The number of addicts remained low, and users were able to take quality-controlled drugs under medical supervision. Moreover, the black market was negligible, and addicts did not have to commit crimes to support their habits.

But then, during the 1960s, heroin use doubled, especially among Britain's youth. With this dramatic growth came a "gray market" in drugs. Addicts would convince their physicians to prescribe more heroin than they needed. The heroin prescribed was relatively low in potency. So addicts would sell their prescription heroin on the gray market ("gray" instead of "black," because what they were selling was originally purchased legally). Then they turned around and bought the more potent heroin that was streaming in from illegal foreign sources.

In response to this trend, the British government adopted a new approach. It denied private physicians the right to prescribe either heroin or methadone (a substitute drug). Instead, addicts were required to register at government-run drug treatment centers (DTCs), where they could obtain their supplies. In addition, the emphasis on treatment was away from long-term maintenance and on short-term maintenance and cure.

Several problems emerged. Addicts who had been comfortable with the old arrangement, with only their physician and pharmacist knowing of their secret habit, were reluctant to register at the government centers. Others were distressed by

47

the government's new policy for short-term maintenance and cure. As a result, many addicts turned to the black market for their drug supplies.

De Facto Legalization
and Decriminalization
De facto legalization and decriminalization are similar. In both cases, the laws against drugs remain on the books; consequently, the drugs remain illegal. De facto legalization overlooks the laws, while decriminalization enforces them, but lessens the penalties for violations. For example, rather than arrest violators of the marijuana laws, violators are cited and fined, much the way traffic violations are considered minor infractions.

Both reforms have the advantage of allowing society to experiment. Then, if the results are unsatisfactory, it is possible to return to enforcing the laws, since they are still intact.

Since nearly half the yearly drug arrests are for marijuana possession, de facto legalization of just marijuana would result in 400,000 fewer arrests.

Either approach takes the burden off law enforcement by freeing officers and agents to concentrate their efforts on big-time traffickers and the hard drugs they push. In addition, both ways send a message that, while some drug use will be tolerated, it is not encouraged.

We already have de facto legalization in other areas of law. Rather than repeal or strike down certain antiquated laws, they are often ignored. Laws that are ignored cover a range of behavior that at one time our society did not tolerate, but now does. For example, the New Hampshire senate recently refused to repeal a 200-year-old law that makes adultery a crime punishable by up to a year in prison. Although the law is no longer enforced, by not striking it down, the senate gave the message that while adultery is not acceptable, it would be tolerated. Laws against astrology, witchcraft, homosexuality, even jaywalking are routinely de facto legalized.

Between 1973 and 1979, eleven states decriminalized the

personal possession of small amounts of marijuana—between one and four ounces, depending on the state. Instead of arrest, violators are given citations and a fine that is usually less than $100.

The state with the most lenient marijuana policy is Alaska. There, the *Ravin* v. *State* decision made it legal to grow and possess marijuana for personal use in the privacy of the home. Adults are permitted to grow up to three cannabis plants per household and to possess up to four ounces of marijuana—the equivalent of 120 joints—without being arrested.

Results of the Alaskan policy are mixed. Law enforcement has been spared the expense and effort of arresting small-time users. On the other hand, Alaskan youths have gotten the message that marijuana is legal and therefore okay, a message that disturbs many Alaskans. Observes Bobi Trani, a middle school substance abuse counselor from Juneau, Alaska: "It's tough to see twelve-year-olds handcuffed and taken from school to the juvenile detention center for bringing to school the pot they took from a drawer at home."[3]

De Facto Legalization:
The Dutch Model
The Dutch have a unique approach to drug abuse. In fact, they are an example of de facto legalization that appears to be working—given their perspective.

In contrast to our zero tolerance policy, Dutch policy accepts that drug use is part of our times, and, moreover, that drug abuse is unavoidable.

The Dutch do not treat their addicts like criminals. Instead, chemically dependent citizens are perceived as members of Dutch society with health problems. That means that although they may be arrested for crimes like theft or assault, addicts will not be arrested just for using illegal drugs.

Treatment is available on demand, immediately, without the United States' customary six-month wait to enter a treatment program. Those addicts who cannot withdraw from drugs or who are not ready to enter treatment can obtain their supply of heroin or methadone (a drug used to treat heroin addiction) at government treatment centers. Because some addicts won't go to treatment centers, the government goes to them—in buses or vans that are parked on streets where addicts are likely to be found.

Dutch addicts are organized into unions called "junkie bonds." These unions lobby on behalf of all addicts. One of their jobs, for example, has been to help operate clean needle and AIDS advice programs for addicts.[4]

Perhaps the most unusual Dutch drug policy concerns the use of cannabis. In "cannabis cafes" throughout Amsterdam, marijuana can be bought as joints, cookies, or "space cakes."[5] This policy is based on the idea that marijuana users are better off not having to mingle with hard-core drug addicts to obtain the drug. Furthermore, by tolerating cannabis, the Dutch hope to make it "boring" to use.

Results of the Dutch experiment are impressive. Only 4 percent of their young people use marijuana regularly, which is one-tenth the U.S. rate. In addition, only a small percentage of Dutch AIDS victims are intravenous drug users, in contrast to more than one-fourth of all U.S. AIDS victims.[6]

De facto legalization works for the Netherlands in part because Dutch addicts are not outside the mainstream but rather are within it. Eddy L. Englesman, the Dutch Minister of Health and the director of drug policy, illustrates this attitude when he explains that drug addicts "are part of the Dutch family."

As "part of the family," addicts are eligible for public health care and minimum income guarantees. Unlike the majority of U.S. addicts, Dutch addicts are able to maintain standards of living above poverty.

Because there are so many cultural differences between the United States and the Netherlands, it is difficult to draw an exact parallel between their drug policy and ours. What works for them may not work for us. Nonetheless, the Dutch model stands alone as an example of drug reform that neither increases drug use nor declares civil war.

A RIGHT OR A RIDICULOUS IDEA?

A war on drugs is a good idea, but not if its first casualty is the Bill of Rights.
—Attorney General of Maryland

Drugs laws fail to stop drug use. And while they try to stop it, they create new problems. These are the reasons most critics want to change drug laws. A few, however, are concerned about drug laws for other reasons.

Libertarians are people who are concerned about protecting civil rights. They believe that the drug laws infringe on the right to privacy. They also believe that the way drug laws are enforced, from wiretapping and random drug testing to warrantless searches, erodes civil rights.

THE RIGHT TO USE DRUGS

Imagine a person who has nurtured several marijuana plants in a greenhouse adjacent to his house. He harvests some of the leaves. When they are dry, he cleans them. Before storing the marijuana in his nightstand, he rolls some into a few joints.

That evening he goes to a concert with his friends. In the car on the way to the concert, they light up the joints. A plainclothes detective in a car near theirs sees them. At the next traffic light, he arrests them, charging them with possession of marijuana.

Since 1965, over eight million people have been arrested for a marijuana crime.[1] Four hundred thousand will be arrested this year for possession of marijuana. Does society have the right to outlaw their behavior? Is it in our best interest to arrest, convict, even jail them?

In their lifetimes, more than sixty million people have tried marijuana; thirty million smoked it during the past year.[2] Trying it even once has put some of them into the limelight—and out of a career.

In 1987 Douglas H. Ginsberg was nominated as a Supreme Court justice. He would have made history as the youngest justice ever to serve on the country's highest court. Instead, he made history as the first nominee to be rejected for having smoked marijuana. When word got out that he had tried marijuana during his student days, there was such a public uproar that Ginsberg felt compelled to decline the nomination.

Another victim of drug laws was Washington, D.C.'s mayor, Marion Berry. In 1990, he was arrested for illicit drug use during a federal investigation of public corruption.

CIVIL LIBERTIES

What right does government have to decide what we can and cannot do? In 1859, in his famous essay *On Liberty,* John Stuart Mill advised free societies and their governments to protect the individual's rights. Wrote Mill: "The only purpose for which power can be rightfully exercised over any member of a civilized community, against his will, is to prevent harm to others. His own good," he continued, "either physical or moral, is not a sufficient warrant."[3]

In a free society, people take many risks. They smoke cigarettes, race bobsleds, hang-glide, or climb Mount Everest without breaking the law. Reflecting on Mill's advice, Stephen

Wisotsky, a legal scholar, claims that "a democratic society must respect the decisions made by its adult citizens, even those perceived as foolish or risky."[4]

"Paternalism" is a term used for laws that are passed to protect citizens from harm. One example of paternalism is seat belt laws. According to the Department of Transportation, if all automobile passengers used seat belts, 10,000 lives would be saved each year.[5] To protect their citizens, thirty-two states have enacted laws requiring drivers and passengers to buckle up.[6]

If the occasional use of drugs like marijuana or cocaine gives users pleasure, what right does society have to say they can't use them? And if some people abuse drugs, is that enough reason to prevent the millions who don't from using them?

Remember that over 70 million Americans have tried illegal drugs. In 1988 alone, nearly fourteen million did.[7] Does our government have the right to legislate morality or to maintain laws that make criminals out of so many of its citizens?

John Kaplan, author of a book about heroin addiction, admits that Mill's advice that government should stay out of private affairs is appealing. "But it does not work in the real world," suggests Kaplan, "where a cyclist without a helmet can crash and end up the public's ward in some nursing home."[8] Thus, if the public has to provide food, shelter, and medical help to addicts who are too down and out to provide for themselves, should society pass laws to prevent addiction in the first place?

THE MEDICAL USE OF DRUGS
THAT ARE BANNED

New research on marijuana indicates that it might be a useful drug to treat pain, insomnia (inability to sleep), anxiety (nervousness), epilepsy, asthma, glaucoma, and the vomiting resulting from chemotherapy. However, marijuana is strictly scheduled and available (by prescription) in only about thirty

53

states. Furthermore, because it must be purchased through the government, the prescriptions for it are often easier to obtain than the marijuana itself.

In 1975, Bob Randall, a Washington, D.C., resident, was arrested and charged with unlawful possession of marijuana. The reason? His use of marijuana to treat glaucoma, a disease of the eye that causes blindness.

Randall took his case to court, but it was dismissed. The judge ruled that anyone who needs marijuana for medical treatment is not criminally liable for possessing it. In effect, the judge affirmed Randall's right to protect his health. That right, however, does not extend to pain relief.

Each year, about 8,000 cancer patients lie dying in excruciating pain. Though the pain of hundreds of thousands of others is treatable with drugs like Dilaudid and morphine, theirs is not. Heroin might help them, but in the United States, its use is prohibited.

Equal amounts of heroin are more than twice as potent as morphine. Heroin also acts faster, causes less nausea and vomiting, and makes patients calmer. And because it dissolves more readily in liquids, it is less painful an injection.

When heroin was first sold by the Bayer Company in 1898, it was used primarily to treat respiratory illnesses. Then its euphoric qualities became known—and its addictiveness. Heroin is one of the most addictive drugs known.

Because it was cheap and available, heroin became popular among drug addicts. As a result, Congress added it to the list of restricted drugs in 1924, when the Harrison Act was amended.

Although heroin was available as a prescription for pain relief, doctors began to replace it with safer pain relievers. In 1960, when Jefferson Hospital in Philadelphia was denied permission to continue using heroin, it turned its remaining supply over to the federal government. Jefferson was the last hospital in the United States to use heroin.

Heroin has always been used for pain relief in hospices in Great Britain. Despite the excellent results in Great Britain, the United States has remained steadfast in its ban of the drug. When the Controlled Substance Act was passed in 1970, Attorney General John Mitchell had the opportunity to place heroin in Schedule II (which would have allowed doctors to prescribe it), but he failed to do so.

To persuade Congress to reschedule heroin, the National Committee for the Treatment of Intractable Pain, headed by Judith Quattlebaum, was founded. The committee was able to convince a few senators and congressmen to sponsor bills to make heroin available to dying cancer patients.

The first bill was the Compassionate Pain Relief Act, introduced by Representative Henry Waxman. However, in 1984, following hours of passionate debate, the bill was overwhelmingly defeated by a 355–55 House vote.

The bill was introduced again, this time by Senator Daniel Inouye. Again it met defeat.

Resistance to the bill focused on the belief that there are better alternatives to heroin. In addition, there was the fear that the medical supply of heroin would be stolen from hospitals and ultimately sold on the street.

John D. Dingell, chairman of the congressional committee that had reported favorably on the bill, satirized that fear when he said: "Let us take a little bit of a look at the question . . . 4.3 tons of illegal heroin come into this country. That is the equivalent of two elephants in weight. If you were to take the entire amount of heroin that is going to be coming into this country under carefully controlled conditions to meet the needs of the hopelessly dying cancer patients, you would probably have the equivalent of a pimple on the posterior of one of those elephants."[9]

In another commentary on the subject, Smith Hempstone, editor of the *Washington Times*, wrote: "The absolute medical ban on heroin makes about as much sense as denying a man about to be electrocuted a cigarette on the grounds that the Surgeon General has determined smoking is injurious to the health."[10]

FOURTH AMENDMENT RIGHTS

The right of the people to be secure in their persons, houses, papers, and effects, against unreasonable searches and seizures, shall not be violated, and no warrants shall issue, but upon probable cause, supported by oath or affirmation, and particularly describing the place to be searched, and the persons or things to be seized.
—*The Fourth Amendment*

The Fourth Amendment is supposed to protect citizens from unlawful search and seizure. But as the drug war intensifies, the boundaries between lawful and unlawful are being eroded. In fact, recent Supreme Court decisions have raised serious concern about those rights.

Even if only one marijuana plant is discovered, the government has the right to seize 5,000 adjoining acres of land.[11] In fact, it has the right to seize any land or personal property that is involved in drug trafficking.

A couple from Michigan was returning from a Canadian vacation when their car was inspected at the border by U.S. Customs. When the agent found two marijuana joints in the husband's pocket, he confiscated their car.[12] In another example, David Phelps, a shrimp fisherman from Key West, Florida, lost his seventy-three-foot shrimper to the Coast Guard after officials found three grams of cannabis seeds and stems aboard.[13]

According to the Fourth Amendment, law officers are required to obtain a search warrant before checking for drugs. They must legally justify their search in order to obtain one. Yet in the zeal to catch drug abusers, search warrants are no longer always required.

Without search warrants, police are now permitted to search private property, even property surrounded by fences and marked with "no trespassing" signs (*Oliver* v. *United*

States, 1984). They may search a barn that is adjacent to a residence (*United States* v. *Dunn*, 1987).

Without the consent of customers, police may inspect bank records, record telephone numbers dialed from a person's home, and secretly tape telephone and personal, face-to-face conversations. In addition, police may inspect anyone's trash. They may set up roadblocks, stopping all drivers to search their cars, including the glove compartment, trunk, and any briefcases they find inside.

Brownville is a quaint, upscale village in the Midwest. (Its name and the names of the people in the following account have been changed.) Brownville police routinely look through the pharmacy's Schedule II prescription records for signs of drug abuse.[14] Occasionally a prescription looks suspicious to them.

"Why did Dr. Goldberg prescribe a hundred phenobarbitol for Joyce McAllen?" asks one of the officers.

"For her epilepsy," replies the pharmacist, mindful of the drug laws, but irritated by the search.

"This prescription here," continues the officer, *". . . why are there so many Percodan prescriptions for Bob Hart?"*

"His cancer," says the pharmacist.

All over the United States, in communities like Brownville, police routinely search through prescription records, looking for abuse of drugs like Percodan, Dilaudid, Tylox, Zandas, Adipex, and Ritalin.

In states like New York, Schedule II prescriptions are coded into a central computer. To protect their privacy, just the first few letters of the patients' last names and their zip codes are on the computer. From the code, a patient cannot be identified. (If officials are suspicious of drug abuse, they can obtain permission to see the actual name.)

In contrast, Brownville prescriptions were not coded or entered into computers. Officers there recognized many of the names. In fact, because Brownville is such a small town, they knew many of the patients personally.

Do officers have the right to such private information as the kind of medication a citizen takes for an illness? Is finding a few doctors or pharmacists who prescribe or dispense too many drugs worth the trample on civil rights of those who don't abuse drugs? Critics believe such searches are unwarranted and violate the right to privacy. Still, the Supreme Court upheld prescription monitoring.

In another Supreme Court decision involving a low-altitude helicopter search (*Florida* v. *Riley,* 1989), the Court ruled that police may spy for marijuana plants in greenhouses and private property from crafts flying as low as 400 feet. According to the majority opinion, low-altitude spying is not unreasonable, "because low-altitude flying is neither unlawful nor unusual."

Commenting on that decision, Justice William Brennan, one of the four dissenting justices, found the parallel to George Orwell's novel, *Nineteen Eighty-Four,* alarming. " 'In the far distance a helicopter skimmed down between the roofs, hovered for an instant like a bluebottle, and darted away again with a curving flight,' " quoted Brennan from the book. " 'It was the Police Patrol, snooping into people's windows.' "[15]

Brennan's comment: "Who can read this passage without a shudder?"

DRUG TESTING

Drug testing is routinely done on all suspected criminals. In addition, more than 40 percent of Fortune 500 companies—the largest corporations in the U.S.—now test for drugs. So do the federal government, any company with a federal contract, and many smaller companies. There isn't a life insurance company that doesn't require a test for drug use.

The Department of Transportation proposed random drug tests for the airline industry's half a million employees, the railroad's 120,000 workers, and the five million bus and truck drivers. The U.S. Coast Guard proposed testing all 130,000 of its crew members, including all the snack bar workers on the Puget Sound Ferry System.[16]

Drug testing raises several questions. Are they unwarranted searches? Do they invade a person's privacy? Are they accurate? Might not some drugs, like amphetamines, which help users stay awake, or cocaine, which makes users stronger, also improve the performance of certain jobs?

On March 21, 1989, the Supreme Court ruled on drug testing of employees. In the first case, *Skinner* v. *Railway Labor Executives,* the Court upheld the tests as a way to ensure public safety. In the majority opinion, Justice Anthony Kennedy wrote that the tests were indeed "searches." They were reasonable searches, however, because operating rail equipment while drug-impaired, in Kennedy's opinion, is too great a risk to both the passengers and the workers themselves.

But in a dissenting opinion, Justice Thurgood Marshall accused the Court's majority of allowing itself to be "swept away by society's obsession with stopping the scourge of illegal drugs.

"History teaches that grave threats to liberty often come in times of urgency, when constitutional rights seem too extravagant to endure." He continued, "There is no drug exception to the Constitution."

So far, drug tests of the more than 3,600 U.S. Customs agents have turned up only five cases of illegal drug use. However, despite this lack of evidence of widespread drug abuse, in another Supreme Court decision, Justice Kennedy argued that public safety overrides the privacy of U.S. Customs agents. Testing them is acceptable and legal.

Setting aside the privacy issue for a while, another concern is the accuracy of drug testing. Unlike the Breathalyzer tests for alcohol use, urine testing, the method most commonly used for drugs, cannot measure how intoxicated a person is at the time of the test. Nor can it distinguish drug use from drug abuse.

The New York State Appeals Court upheld the legality of

a hair test for a Scarsdale, New York, mother accused of abusing cocaine. She lost custody of her child, even though hair testing for cocaine is still experimental and lacks scientific proof of its accuracy.[17]

Drug testing can indicate that a drug is present in the body. But it may do so long after that person's job performance is affected. For example, someone on vacation can smoke marijuana. When the person returns to work the following Monday morning, he or she will test positive for marijuana use, even though the drug's effects have worn off.

There are certain drugs that are commonly taken for muscle aches or arthritis. These drugs are legal and may be purchased over the counter or with a prescription. Though they have none of the effects of marijuana, they show up as marijuana on the urine test, giving a false report.[18]

Cocaine cannot be detected more than two to four days after it has been consumed. An employee heavily abusing it over the weekend can show up for work, have his urine tested, and the cocaine may go undetected. In contrast, persons using PCP (angel dust) may remain paranoid and delusional days after the drug is detectable.[19]

Finally, it is not unusual for people who use drugs to bring in urine samples that are not their own. Clean vials of urine can be purchased for twenty dollars. For this reason, many urine tests are now being conducted in full view of a supervisor. "Hey," said one irate employee, "how would you like to pee in front of your boss?"

Drug testing may step on civil rights, but is it effective? When the U.S. military discovered widespread drug use among returning Vietnam veterans, it began the first legal urine tests for drugs. Then, in 1981, the military began to test everyone, from recruits to officers.

In 1980, survey results revealed that 27 percent of military personnel were found to have used drugs within the month of the survey. By 1982, the figure was down to 19 percent, and by 1985, after massive drug testing, it was only a third of the original rate—9 percent.[20] Perhaps the constant reminder that a positive urine test may cost them their jobs is enough to deter many people from using or abusing drugs.

Is the success of drug testing worth the erosion of civil rights? Yes, voted the Supreme Court, though not unanimously. Antonin Scalia, a dissenting justice in the U.S. Customs Agency decision, believes that unreasonable searches can never be justified, regardless of how worthy the cause to conduct them may be.

6

THE BILLION-DOLLAR BUSINESS

How can you place a dollar value on the wasted lives, shattered careers, and broken homes legalization would bring?
        —John Lawn, head of the Drug
            Enforcement Agency (DEA)

Cash. Illegal drugs earn cash. Cash that is in fives, tens, twenties, and hundreds. Small denominations, but amounts so large they cannot be counted. Instead, they are sorted by denominations and weighed.

Drugs are a billion-dollar industry. Americans spent more than $110 billion dollars on them in 1989,[1] an amount exceeding the gross national income of 150 of the 170 nations of the world.[2]

In 1988, the Drug Enforcement Administration toppled a crack empire known as the Chambers Brothers organization. The Chambers Brothers drug group controlled half the crack houses in Detroit and was run like a professional business. The "company" had over 500 employees, quality-control checks on its product, even sales competitions to motivate its workers.

The company's sales figures were as remarkable as its business acumen. Chambers Brothers netted between $1 million and $3 million every single day.

In another drug bust in Los Angeles, thirty-three people and their corporation were charged with laundering more than $500 million in Colombian cocaine profits. They had hidden the illegal source of their money through jewelry merchants in Los Angeles, Texas, Florida, and New York. According to the Justice and Treasury departments, in just two years the group had laundered a billion dollars in drug money.

The allure of such wealth attracts people from ghetto youth to middle-aged wealthy suburbanites. In 1989, a couple from Roslyn, Long Island, were arrested and charged with running a money-laundering operation that had transported more than $350 million to a drug cartel in Colombia.

For five years sociologist Terry Williams took a close look at teenage drug dealers in New York's Spanish Harlem. Through the drug trade these youths were able to make a fantastic living and obtain status, prestige, and proof of success. They worked long, hard hours, often seven days a week.

"Selling coke is just like any other business," explained one youthful dealer. "You gotta work long hours, stay on your toes, protect what's yours," and he added, "not mess with 'silly matters.' "

The rewards for hustling earn young dealers as much as $2,500 for a day's work. Sometimes it is their only opportunity to earn a decent living.

One sixteen-year-old girl from Queens, New York, held a typical part-time job dealing drugs, a job that was hardly competition for any legitimate job she might have had. With assistance from two lookouts and two helpers, Lyvia sold crack. She dressed in her church clothes, as she explained, "so that the police would not suspect me."

From a male dealer, Lyvia would receive $500 worth of crack, an amount she easily sold out in half an hour on a weekend night. She only worked twice a week, though for twelve hours at a stretch. For every $500 Lyvia sold, she was permitted to keep only $25. But those $25 quickly accumulated. Each night, Lyvia sold $12,000 worth of crack, and each week she earned $1,200 (most of which went toward drugs for herself).

Even the lookouts, whose job it is to warn dealers of police officers or DEA agents, earn more money than they could at any legitimate job. They can earn $75 to $100 a day[3]—no small change for a ten-year-old.

Opportunity abounds for drug runners, or "mules" as they are called in the trade. Along the U.S. border with Mexico, drugs are often transported by mules who may walk as far as fifty miles with their loads on their backs before reaching their contact. Their compensation is $250 to $1,000 a load, substantial earnings for many of the poor Mexicans who carry the loads.[4]

The best paid runners are pilots. A pilot transporting illicit cargo in a twin-engine plane can command up to $200,000 to drop a load across the Mexican border into Texas, California, New Mexico, or Arizona. Transports from Colombia in turbo jets fetch their pilots as much as a half million dollars per flight.

The greatest wealth has been accumulated by the biggest drug dealers, those members of the drug cartels in Latin America. In 1989, when the Colombian government impounded more than $200 million worth of property during a massive weekend roundup of 11,000 suspects, officials found vast fortunes. Cartel members were living in lavish ranches replete with gold-plated faucets, imported marble and crystal, squash courts, and indoor swimming pools. One pool was outfitted with artificial grass. Besides stables with purebred horses, there was even a 1,000-acre zoo on a private island owned by the Ochoa clan, a major force in the drug cartel.

MONEY LAUNDERING

Because selling drugs is not a legitimate business, all the transactions are done in cash. But it is not cash that is always easy to spend. Some of it goes toward flashy clothes, shoes, cars, and other luxuries. One fourteen-year-old dealer in

Washington, D.C., parks his shiny black Porsche in his tenement parking lot.

Spending too much in cash, however, can arouse the attention of the Internal Revenue Service law enforcement agents. Before this money can be spent, it must be converted to an account of a business that won't attract attention. This is called money laundering, and it can require a sophisticated knowledge of high finance.

The Internal Revenue Service, which audits banks, has set up safeguards against money laundering. One of the major safeguards is a rule that any bank receiving a deposit over $10,000 must report the deposit to the IRS. Ten thousand dollars may seem like a lot of money, but to a drug operation receiving a million dollars a day, that's a hundred deposits— for one day. Just counting those enormous quantities of cash is a Herculean task.

Since American banks have to report large deposits, many drug operators have the money transported out of the country and into foreign banks willing to cooperate, or at least willing to keep their transactions private.

All this counting, transporting, and laundering of money is quite a challenge—one a number of enterprising people are bribed or lured into accepting.

In one of its largest money-laundering busts ever, an undercover DEA agent with the assumed name Bobby Musella posed as a money launderer. Musella won the trust of drug dealers and bankers willing to cooperate. When Musella invited them to his phony wedding to Kathleen Erickson (another undercover agent), they accepted, eager to attend the affair.

Guests were put up at a swank hotel near Tampa, Florida. On the day before the "wedding," DEA agents circulated among the male guests, inviting them to a stag party to be held in downtown Tampa that evening. When the guests were picked up in a fleet of limousines, they were surprised to find that instead of attending the stag party, they were delivered to federal agents who handcuffed and arrested them.

Operation C-Chase, as the sting was dubbed, successfully indicted eighty-four people. Thirty-two million dollars in drug money was retrieved through the money laundering. But $32 million pales next to the 200 million to 300 million drug dollars that change hands in the United States every day.

COST OF THE
WAR ON DRUGS

Money is one of the loudest arguments voiced by those who want to legalize drugs. Conservative economist Milton Friedman sums up this argument when he states frankly, "The war on drugs is too expensive." Legalization, he believes, makes economic sense.

Catching drug criminals takes manpower. Police spend days sitting in their patrol cars, surveilling the comings and goings of suspects before they can gather enough evidence for searches or arrests. One typical drug bust in Cleveland required forty agents and officers to bust just three apartments. All this costs taxpayers money.

How much is too much money? According to a U.S. Customs study prepared by Wharton Econometrics, state and local police agencies use one-fifth of their budgets on drug law enforcement.[5] This amounts to nearly $5 billion, and that does not include what the federal government spends. In 1988, it spent nearly $4 billion fighting the drug war, and in 1989, William Bennett, the new drug czar, had proposed nearly doubling that amount.

There is an acute shortage of jails and prisons to house all the convicted drug felons. In places like New York City, the shortage is critical. Mark Kleinman of Harvard projects that building enough new ones may cost state and federal governments up to $50 billion.[6] Just to hold one convicted person on drug charges before the case ever goes to court costs taxpayers several thousand dollars. Locking the person away if he's convicted and sentenced can run as much as $50,000.[7]

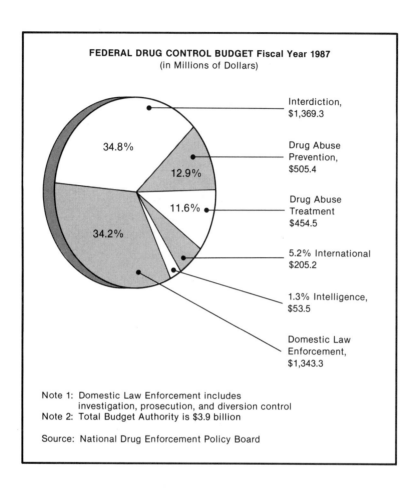

FEDERAL DRUG CONTROL BUDGET Fiscal Year 1987
(in Millions of Dollars)

34.8%

12.9%

11.6%

34.2%

Interdiction,
$1,369.3

Drug Abuse
Prevention,
$505.4

Drug Abuse
Treatment
$454.5

5.2% International
$205.2

1.3% Intelligence,
$53.5

Domestic Law
Enforcement,
$1,343.3

Note 1: Domestic Law Enforcement includes
investigation, prosecution, and diversion control
Note 2: Total Budget Authority is $3.9 billion

Source: National Drug Enforcement Policy Board

It may be worth tax dollars to catch big-time dealers, drug runners, even those who sell drugs to minors. But is it worth the $1,200 it costs to arrest and convict a person for using marijuana?

THE COST OF DRUG USE

Obviously, the billions spent enforcing the drug laws could be saved if drugs were legalized, but would those savings be offset by the cost of drug use, and especially drug abuse? Who is going to pay for treatment and prevention programs? Will the taxpayers foot the bill? The Federal Alcohol, Drug Abuse, and Mental Health Administration estimates that each year drug users cost business and industry $100 million.

In 1985, a computer operator for a major airline was high on marijuana, so high that he forgot to load an essential tape into the computer that the airline used for reservations. The result of his neglect was an eight-hour breakdown in service. The cost to the airline? Nineteen million dollars!

Drug testing is supposed to prevent mishaps like this one. But it, too, has a price tag, costing business and industry thousands of dollars.

IF DRUGS ARE LEGALIZED,
THEY CAN BE TAXED

When liquor and cigarettes are sold, they are taxed, and the public benefits from those taxes. In contrast, drug laws deprive the public of taxation on illegal drug sales and their profits.

A few states have actually imposed taxation on illegal drug sales. In September 1989, Texas enacted what is known as the "Al Capone Law." (Capone, the famous Prohibition bootlegger, was nabbed on tax evasion, not bootlegging charges.) Dealers are required to buy a tax "stamp" that costs $3,500 for marijuana and $100,000 for cocaine. Then they are expected to pay taxes on what they sell, which amounts to $3.50 per gram of marijuana and $200 per gram of cocaine.[8]

Of course, no officials expect drug dealers to voluntarily pay taxes, but they do expect to use the tax against dealers who are arrested and convicted of drug charges. Twelve other states have similar laws. Though few enforce the law, together Minnesota, Florida, and Arizona have collected a total of over a million dollars in back taxes, with millions more in delinquent taxes on the books.

If drugs were legalized, predicts Dr. Lester Grinspoon of Harvard, upwards of $10 billion in tax revenues could be

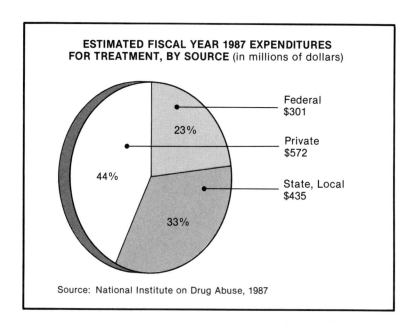

**ESTIMATED FISCAL YEAR 1987 EXPENDITURES
FOR TREATMENT, BY SOURCE** (in millions of dollars)

Federal
$301

Private
$572

State, Local
$435

23%

44%

33%

Source: National Institute on Drug Abuse, 1987

collected from legal drug sales. He suggests that these revenues could then be spent on treatment and prevention programs.

Optimistic? Perhaps. If drugs were legalized, most experts, including Dr. Grinspoon, agree that the number of addicts could increase, to as many as twenty million. If that occurs, can $10 billion in tax revenues offset the cost of treating millions of addicts, not to mention the cost of prevention programs?

Probably not at current costs. Residential treatment costs about $70 a day.[9] Given the fact that many addicts require lengthy or repeated treatment, the bill for twenty million addicts would be staggering—as high as $30 billion—or three times what Dr. Grinspoon speculates would be raised from taxes. Who will pay the deficit?

If drugs themselves are taxed to cover it, their prices will be too high; a new black market in cheaper drugs could emerge (or users would once again turn to cheaper, possibly more

Federal Trafficking Penalties—Marijuana   Narcotics Penalties & Enforcement Act of 1986

Quantity	Description	First Offense	Second Offense
1,000 kg or more	**Marijuana** Mixture containing detectable quantity*	Not less than 10 years, not more than life. If death or serious injury, not less than 20 years, not more than life. Fine not more than $4 million individual, $10 million other than individual.	Not less than 20 years, not more than life. If death or serious injury, not less than life. Fine not more than $8 million individual, $20 million other than individual.
100 kg to 1,000 kg	**Marijuana** Mixture containing detectable quantity*	Not less than 5 years, not more than 40 years. If death or serious injury, not less than 20 years, not more than life. Fine not more than $2 million individual, $5 million other than individual.	Not less than 10 years, not more than life. If death or serious injury, not less than life. Fine not more than $4 million individual, $10 million other than individual.
50 to 100 kg	**Marijuana**	Not more than 20 years. If death or serious injury, not less than 20 years, not more than life. Fine $1 million individual, $5 million other than individual.	Not more than 30 years. If death or serious injury, life. Fine $2 million individual, $10 million other than individual.
10 to 100 kg	**Hashish**		
1 to 100 kg	**Hashish Oil**		
100 or more plants	**Marijuana**		
Less than 50 kg	**Marijuana**	Not more than 5 years. Fine not more than $250,000, $1 million other than individual.	Not more than 10 years. Fine $500,000 individual, $2 million other than individual.
Less than 10 kg	**Hashish**		
Less than 1 kg	**Hashish Oil**		

*Includes hashish and hash oil

(Marijuana is a Schedule I controlled substance.)

Federal Trafficking Penalties

Narcotics Penalties & Enforcement Act of 1986

CSA	PENALTY 2nd Offense	PENALTY 1st Offense	Quantity	DRUG	Quantity	PENALTY 1st Offense	PENALTY 2nd Offense
I	Not less than 10 years. Not more than life. If death or serious injury, not less than life. Fine of not more than $4 million individual, $10 million other than individual.	Not less than 5 years. Not more than 40 years. If death or serious injury, not less than 20 years. Not more than life. Fine of not more than $2 million individual, $5 million other than individual.	100-999 gm mixture	HEROIN	1 kg or more mixture	Not less than 10 years. Not more than life. If death or serious injury, not less than 20 years. Not more than life. Fine of not more than $4 million individual, $10 million other than individual.	Not less than 20 years. Not more than life. If death or serious injury, not less than life. Fine of not more than $8 million individual, $20 million other than individual.
I			500-4,999 gm mixture	COCAINE	5 kg or more mixture		
and			5-49 gm mixture	COCAINE BASE	50 gm or more mixture		
and			10-99 gm or 100-999 gm mixture	PCP	100 gm or more or 1 kg or more mixture		
II	Fine of not more than $4 million individual, $10 million other than individual.	Fine of not more than $2 million individual, $5 million other than individual.	1-10 gm mixture	LSD	10 gm or more mixture	Fine of not more than $4 million individual, $10 million other than individual.	Fine of not more than $8 million individual, $20 million other than individual.
II			40-399 gm mixture	FENTANYL	400 gm or more mixture		
II			10-99 gm mixture	FENTANYL ANALOGUE	100 gm or more mixture		

CSA	Drug	Quantity	First Offense	Second Offense
	Others*	Any	Not more than 20 years. If death or serious injury, not less than 20 years, not more than life. Fine $1 million individual, $5 million not individual.	Not more than 30 years. If death or serious injury, life. Fine $2 million individual, $10 million not individual.
III	All	Any	Not more than 5 years. Fine not more than $250,000 individual, $1 million not individual.	Not more than 10 years. Fine not more than $500,000 individual, $2 million not individual.
IV	All	Any	Not more than 3 years. Fine not more than $250,000 individual, $1 million not individual.	Not more than 6 years. Fine not more than $500,000 individual, $2 million not individual.
V	All	Any	Not more than 1 year. Fine not more than $100,000 individual, $250,000 not individual.	Not more than 2 years. Fine not more than $200,000 individual, $500,000 not individual.

*Does not include marijuana, hashish, or hashish oil. (See separate chart.)

dangerous drugs). Higher taxation and drug prices would also defeat one of the reasons for legalizing drugs in the first place—to make them affordable so users don't have to steal or deal for them.

Nor can tax revenues begin to cover the cost in human misery. In recent studies of pregnant women, researchers found that 10 percent of all pregnant women are using illegal drugs during their pregnancy. In the inner city, the rate is even higher—one study found that 20 percent of all the women who were pregnant were using cocaine.[10]

Babies born to these mothers are frequently premature. Many suffer withdrawal at birth, as well as lifelong damage to their health and learning abilities. While such suffering has no dollar measurement, the babies' medical care does. It costs $80,000 to detoxify a crack-addicted baby at birth, and between $100,000 to $150,000 to care for them if they are born prematurely.[11]

LEGALIZATION WOULD REDUCE
THE PRICE OF DRUGS

"Chippers" are people who use illicit drugs occasionally. Because they don't use drugs often, they can usually afford to pay for them. It is people who are dependent on drugs who cannot afford them. Compared to cigarette addiction or alcoholism, drug habits are expensive.

A drug habit can cost hundreds, even thousands, of dollars a week. Such costs are beyond the reach of most addicts, unless they engage in illicit sources of income. There are few legitimate jobs available, especially to poor, uneducated youth, that can support $500-a-week habits. For the most part, addicts are too young, too unskilled, or too burnt out to hold legitimate jobs. They may also be criminals who don't want honest work. Regardless of why they can't afford drugs, addicts become desperate for them anyway.

Even wealthy addicts may find drug habits too costly. At the Benjamin Rush Center in Syracuse, New York, Dr. Ronald J. Dougherty treated a wealthy young man addicted to cocaine. Dr. Dougherty tells this man's riches-to-rags saga:

> *By the age of twenty-six, he had become a millionaire. Once he began freebasing cocaine, he could not stop. He'd line up one pipe after another, in a row, and freebase until the pipe got so hot he had to put it down.*
>
> *Eventually, this young fellow lost his business, his condominium, and his expensive sports car. In the four months before he entered our treatment program, he had consumed over $200,000 worth of cocaine. Yet he was barely able to hold down a job as a dishwasher in a diner.*

LEGALIZATION WOULD DRIVE ORGANIZED CRIME OUT OF THE DRUG BUSINESS

To users, the appeal of drugs is getting high. But for those who produce or sell drugs, it is money they're after. Few products rival the profit on drugs, which can exceed 5,000 times a drug's original costs.

Cleveland Detective Dan Zaller explains why drugs are so lucrative. A fellow bought $600 worth of cocaine in Detroit. He broke this cocaine into 100 pieces of crack. Then he drove to Cleveland, where he sold each "rock" for $25. This netted him $2,500, a profit of nearly $2,000.

Says Zaller, "He will return to Detroit, invest the money in more crack, and within a month see a $75,000 profit on his sales."

Drugs cost little to produce, but the return on their investment is incredible. For example, in 1987, a pound of marijuana sold for $6 to $11 on Colombian beaches and airstrips. By the time it arrived on U.S. soil, however, it sold for $550 to $990.[12] In 1989, a pound of cocaine cost $700 in Bogota. In New York, that same pound sold for $5,000, and in Paris

73

it fetched as much as $12,000.[13] What accounts for these enormous increases?

The increase, or markup, is due to what experts call a "crime tariff." This is what the sellers add to the cost of illegal goods to make it worth the risk they must take in order to sell them—a steep risk at that.

Selling drugs is not only dangerous because of all the battles over turf (on the average, three drug dealers are murdered each day in the U.S.), but also because of the penalties imposed for breaking the law.[14] Although many drug dealers are lucky enough to get away with only parole, others get lifetime sentences with no parole.

To make it worth those risks, sellers substantially increase the price of drugs. Legal drugs would not be risky to sell and would therefore carry no crime tariff. Indeed, if they were legal, they would probably be no more profitable than alcohol or cigarettes are now. On the other hand, they would have to be profitable enough to attract legitimate businesses. Would those businesses then advertise and try to lure people into buying their products?

When alcohol was legalized, it was no longer profitable, and organized crime left the market. Legalizing drugs would probably have the same effect, driving the illegitimate producers and dealers out of business.

On the other hand, as legalized gambling (state lotteries) has shown, criminals who grow attached to the profits find resourceful ways of competing with legitimate business. By increasing the odds or filling odd niches, they stay in the business and stay in it illegally.

Given the enormous profits and the fierce determination to stay in the drug trade that the Medellín and Cali cartels have already shown in Colombia, it is doubtful that drug lords will let legalization pave their way to retirement.

When Prohibition ended, Seagrams, a Canadian distillery that had supplied liquor to the American black market, was suddenly able to supply it legally. In fact, Seagrams became an industry leader.

It is possible, if not conceivable, that legalization would allow drug dealers to go the same route as Seagrams. But it is only a gamble that they would follow suit, and it may be too dangerous a bet to wager.

PRODUCING DRUGS

Selling drugs is not the only gold mine. Producing them has tremendous gains as well.

Take coca plants. Once planted, they grow for thirty, even forty, years and yield up to six crops each year. Few agricultural crops can compete with that kind of success, or profitability.

About one-third of the marijuana consumed in this country is grown here. Most of the other illegal crops such as heroin, cocaine, and crack come from foreign nations, particularly Latin American and Far Eastern countries.

In Latin America, cocaine and marijuana exports gross at least $2 billion in foreign currency each year. Bolivia alone, the poorest of the Latin American nations, earns $600 million from coca production; about 400,000 Bolivians depend on it for their livelihood.[15]

Poor farmers growing illicit crops often find it is the only way to survive economically. For example, wage earners in the Huallaga region of Peru, which produces about a half billion dollars' worth of cocaine, earn only $12 a day. Nevertheless, their wages are as much as eight times what other Peruvian farm workers earn.[16]

Sometimes the farmers have no other choice. If they fail to cooperate, the drug cartels seriously threaten the farmers' and their families' lives. Convincing farmers to give up their lucrative, illicit crops is a dismal prospect. One strategy is to pay them subsidies to grow legal, but less profitable crops. Another has been to destroy their illicit crops through eradication programs.

If drugs are legalized, Mexico, Colombia and other foreign nations could eventually lose out to United States competition, particularly in the marijuana market. But plants like coca grow best in the high altitudes and weather conditions found in those countries already producing illicit drugs. While those countries could continue to supply them if legal, the illicit crops may be no more profitable than tobacco or coffee already is, and may even be less so.

In addition, a competitive world market for drugs will produce cheap prices. Low market prices do not fetch farmers high profits, so legalization may not be able to lift these peasants out of their poverty the way illicit crops do. Nor can it protect them from being exploited as an inexpensive source of drug crops.

Cooperating nations have programs to stamp out the supply of illegal drugs, from killing the crops to destroying the illegal laboratories that process them. Colombia is even trying to engage in a program to destroy the dozens of illegal dirt airstrips used for transporting drugs.

More constructive programs have given peasants incentives to stop producing illegal crops. More often, though, with U.S. cooperation, foreign governments have tried to destroy the crops. Millions of plants have been torn from the earth or killed with herbicides like paraquat.

Losing their only decent source of income is troubling to the peasant farmers. And troubling to government officials. Warned Bolivian President Víctor Paz Estenssoro, "Troops and herbicides may seem like the easiest way to face the problem, but there would be a high cost in social and economic terms. If we cut off the peasants' incomes, they will react, and we want to avoid violence."[17]

DRUG LAWS KEEP THE PRICE OF DRUGS OUT OF REACH

A major goal of drug enforcement is to reduce the supply of illicit drugs on the streets. In fact, drug enforcement officials often measure their success by the street price. The idea is that if the price is too high, it deters people from buying drugs, either because they can't afford them or because they are unwilling to pay such high prices for them.

Sometimes law enforcement is successful. For example, in recent years government agencies cut off so much of the supply of heroin that it became more expensive and more difficult to buy. This probably contributed to stemming the most recent heroin epidemic (one that still left nearly half a million people addicted).

Unfortunately, crackdowns can backfire. Drugs can become so expensive and so difficult to obtain that users are compelled to turn to less expensive alternatives. The less expensive drugs may prove to be even more dangerous and addictive than the original ones.

After the 1909 ban on opium, for example, its price rose. By 1917, opium sold outside the United States for only $20 a tin, but on U.S. soil the price was triple that. By 1924, the price had jumped to $200.[18] Opium was also difficult to find. What did opium smokers turn to? They substituted morphine and heroin, which were cheaper and more plentiful, for the opium.

Another problem with high prices is that if users are paying them, they want more ''kick'' for their money. Instead of settling for weaker drugs, they want stronger ones.

Although the crack epidemic is largely the result of a widespread surplus of cocaine, some experts place part of the blame for it on the high price of marijuana. When law enforcement was successful at driving up the price of marijuana, many drug users, particularly in the ghetto, turned to crack, which was cheaper, more available, and, unfortunately, more addictive.

If drugs were legal, they would be less costly and more affordable. On the other hand, legal drugs could be so inexpensive and so available that, like cigarettes and alcohol, more young people could afford to use them.

In 1983, when crack first appeared on American streets, a vial sold for $50. By the end of the decade, the market was

77

glutted with crack. No matter how much was confiscated by law enforcement agents—and between 10 percent and 20 percent of it was confiscated—the price continued to plummet. By 1989, crack sold for as little as $5 a vial. Those prices attracted more buyers, more users, more abusers.

When the market is glutted with illegal drugs, prices drop. When prices drop, more people can afford to buy drugs. As more people buy them, the demand for the drugs increases. Suppliers try to meet that demand and produce even more drugs. Legalization may reduce the price of drugs, but it does little to reduce the demand for them, and, in fact, may even increase it. This appears to be an economic gamble few Americans want to take.

Economics is one way to justify legalizing drugs. But getting criminals out of the business may be a stretch of the imagination, for criminals have always found ways to satisfy their greed. If drugs are legalized, organized crime and other drug dealers might exit the market. But they are not about to join the Chamber of Commerce.

Many were already crooks when they started dealing drugs. Others are used to the fast dollars and exciting lifestyle, and will probably enter other black markets. Or they may find new ways to exploit the old markets, such as selling drugs to minors.

Legalization would cut the billion-dollar law enforcement bill and ease the burden on the justice system. Billions of dollars in tax revenues could be raised for treatment and prevention. Given the cost of treatment as well as the cost of drug use in general, from crack-dependent babies to lost production, however, most experts agree that tax revenues are offset by other costs.

Some costs cannot be measured. A purely economic approach to the drug war ignores the other side of the equation—the human side. Dollars gained from legalization may pale next to the misery and loss of human potential.

We already spend billions on the drug war. But maybe we are not spending enough. The Medellín cartel in Colombia is probably the largest crime organization in the world (and certainly the most ruthless). They tried to pay off Colombia's $15 billion national debt. Former New York City mayor Ed Koch wryly observed: "The Medellín cartel spends twice as much to stay in the game that we want to end."[19]

7

CAN LEGALIZATION
REDUCE CRIME?

*Alcohol prohibition did not end organized crime.
It just forced a change in product line.*
*—Benjamin Gilman, House
hearings on legalization*

*When legalization is proposed, it is generally out
of frustration with drug-related crime. . . . Any
decrease in violence related to legislation might
be balanced by violent acts committed by people
whose brain chemistry was altered by drugs.*
*—Dr. Charles R. Schuster,
director of the National
Institute on Drug Abuse
(NIDA)*

Huwe Burton was an average sixteen-year-old who attended
school regularly. He earned decent grades. Then he got hooked
on crack. When his mother, a registered nurse, refused to loan
him the $200 he owed a crack dealer, Huwe got angry. He got
so angry, he stabbed his own mother and killed her.

If drugs were the same price as a bottle of wine or a carton
of cigarettes, Huwe might never have murdered his mother.
On the other hand, since he was hooked on crack, he might

80

have gotten just as violent over a different, unrelated issue. We will never know.

The legalization debate requires a careful look at crime. How much crime is generated by people dealing drugs, how much because people are under the influence of drugs, how much by the drug laws themselves? Only when we try to answer these questions can we ask: If drugs were legalized, would there be more or less crime?

As we learned in previous chapters, illicit drug use is common. Among the millions of users and abusers are otherwise law-abiding citizens. Yet because it is illegal to use illicit drugs, each one is guilty of committing a crime.

John DeLorean was starting up an automobile manufacturing plant in Ireland. He needed to raise millions of dollars for it. He worked long days, sometimes getting as little as four hours' sleep. He was constantly on the telephone, in meetings, or traveling. To keep up his stamina, he snorted cocaine. To relax, he smoked marijuana.

DeLorean was busted by U.S. narcotics agents who caught him buying cocaine. At his trial, in his defense, he claimed entrapment. The jury believed him and he was acquitted. But his life was left in shambles. His wife, his business, and his reputation were gone. Worse, even though he had been acquitted, he was branded a lawbreaker by the public.

Drug laws, not drugs, are why John DeLorean was arrested, arrested like anyone else who gets caught using illegal drugs. Arrested like Kevin Mack, a running back for the Cleveland Browns football team. In 1989, Mack faced an eighteen-month prison term and a $2,500 fine after pleading guilty to using crack.

Each year, nearly 400,000 citizens are arrested for possession of marijuana. In 1989, another half million were arrested for drug-related crimes.[1] Does the war against drugs justify so many arrests?

Indeed, a number of people who use drugs are guilty of other crimes. In a recent survey, four out of five state prison

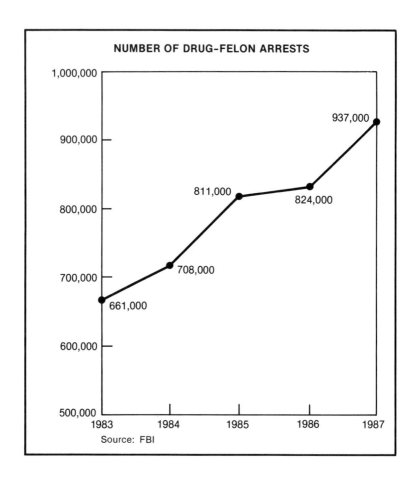

NUMBER OF DRUG-FELON ARRESTS

Source: FBI

inmates admitted to using drugs prior to their arrest, and three out of five had been using drugs regularly.[2] Moreover, inmates who used drugs committed more than their share of crime.

In a study among California inmates, researchers found that drug users committed five times more thefts than non-drug users, while heroin addicts committed fifteen to twenty times more serious offenses.[3]

Much of the overall crime in America is linked to drugs. Nationwide, especially in cities, drug-related crime is on the rise. In New York City, for example, in one year, drug-related crime rose from 24 percent to 40 percent of all crime.[4] And no wonder. Over 600,000 cocaine or crack addicts live in New York.

Hardest hit by drug crime is the nation's capital, Washington, D.C. There, every sixteen hours, someone is murdered because of drugs.[5]

Big cities like New York have no monopoly on drug crimes, however. In Hartford, Connecticut, a medium-sized city, crime rates tripled in two years. And Hartford police estimated that almost all the murders in 1989 were connected to drug use or drug dealing.

Once peaceful neighborhoods and apartment buildings have become unwilling hosts to crack dealers and violent gangs. Two California gangs, the Bloods and the Crips, established drug networks all over the Midwest. Starting from Los Angeles, they have invaded midwestern cities such as Omaha, St. Louis, and Cincinnati. They sell crack. They sell it cheaply. And they are armed to kill anyone who gets in their way.

Other gangs have joined the illegal drug market. Jamaican gangs called "posses" have around 10,000 members distributing crack throughout the United States. In 1988, law enforcement authorities linked these posses to over 1,400 drug-related murders.[6]

Dealers are bolder than ever; they blatantly sell their wares right out on the street, in what police now refer to as "open-air bazaars." They also fight over turf.

Explained a New York gang member being secretly videotaped by police (as he sipped champagne and talked of his trade): "We sell drugs and we kill."

*　　*　　*

Because drug crime is so rampant, many city dwellers fear the neighborhoods where they live, regardless of what time of day it is. That's because drugs are sold around the clock.

Walter Miller lives in a home that only a decade ago was safe. "You could keep your door unlocked," he recalled.

83

"Now, I lock it even when I'm in my yard and can watch it. My dining room faces the street. I don't sit in there at night anymore with the lights on. There's too much shooting around here. Our biggest fear is getting hit by a stray bullet."[7]

A stray bullet from a drug battle outside her home smashed through Rosemary Stevens's window. Mrs. Stevens was a forty-seven-year-old grandmother. That bullet killed her.

For years, police encouraged citizens to help fight crime in their own neighborhoods. They urged them to form neighborhood watches, and to report crimes, identify suspects, and testify against them. The Washington, D.C., City Council even considered an ordinance requiring all apartment tenants to report drug dealing in their buildings or else face eviction. Even those tenants who took cover indoors every night to stay clear of regular gun battles among drug dealers were expected to comply. The most recent federal drug policy also encourages private citizens to join the fight against drugs.

In the opinion of Lawrence W. Sherman, a criminologist at the University of Maryland, however, it is too much to ask private citizens to aid the fight against crack. "We should not urge citizen volunteers to fight the war on drugs alone. Not even Smokey the bear wants us to rush into forest fires with a garden hose." Despite the risks, some brave citizens try anyway.

Lee Arthur Lawrence owned a grocery store in a Florida neighborhood that was home to him and his family for forty years. For the last five years, Lawrence had battled drugs, chasing pushers out of his parking lot, working with police to catch drug dealers, and visiting schools to lecture on drug abuse. On March 23, 1989, the fifty-one-year-old model citizen was shot to death by drug dealers in a spray of up to thirty bullets.

Like Lawrence, Maria and Carlos Hernandez were watchful citizens. And like him, they took the initiative against drug crime in their neighborhood. Maria, thirty-four, and her husband Carlos, forty-two, were the parents of three children. Their youngest was only three years old. When crack infested their Bushwick neighborhood in Brooklyn, New York, the couple chased dealers from the apartment building they owned.

Although Carlos was shot twice by drug dealers and stabbed by a neighbor he had accused of drug dealing, the couple persisted. Both fed police information about local drug dealers.

Then, on the morning of August 8, 1989, as Maria was dressing for work, a spray of bullets was fired through her bedroom window by a revengeful drug dealer. One bullet hit Maria in the temple. She died six hours later.

DRUGS AND CRIMINAL BEHAVIOR

Legalization cannot prevent all crime associated with drugs. Alcohol is legal. Yet many alcoholics abuse their families, drive recklessly, rape, rob, even murder. The same kinds of crime occur when people abuse certain drugs, particularly mind-altering drugs. That is because drugs can affect users' minds in ways that cause them to be irresponsible or violent. Users may become rash and prone to commit crime, all kinds of crime.

Anabolic steroids are not scheduled drugs, but nevertheless they require a prescription to use. Increasingly, however, they are being sold illegally to athletes trying to put on weight and build more body mass.

Although not all experts agree, many believe that anabolic steroids cause a significant number of regular users to become paranoid or to hallucinate. In some users, the symptoms are so severe that they act out of character for themselves, going into what has been dubbed a " 'roid rage."[8]

Before Matt Jones began using anabolic steroids to improve his weight-lifting skills, his twin brother said that he was a quiet, shy young man. But after thirty weeks of steroids, Matt, who had no previous criminal record and had been happily married for several years, grew irritable and irrational. As he told one of his doctors, "If someone had dared me to jump off a cliff, I would have done it, thinking I could not be injured."[9]

Jones did not jump off a cliff. But one day, when he stopped to make a telephone call while driving to work, he experienced a " 'roid rage" when the store clerk joshed him about the phone call. "You use my phone so much," she kidded, "I ought to start charging for it."

Jones did not think that her comment was funny. Instead, he became obsessed with it, believing that she had belittled him. It bothered him so much that he couldn't sleep that night.

The next morning, still angry, he decided to teach her a lesson. He returned to the store and forced her into his car, "to scare the lady," as he explained later.

Indeed, she was so frightened that when he was compelled to stop the car for some road construction, she escaped, running for safety. Before she found it, though, Jones pulled out a revolver he carried for his job as a security officer and shot her in the spine. She is now a paraplegic for life.

Immediately after his arrest, Jones was taken off steroids. A month later, he had returned to being the mild-mannered person he had been before using steroids.

Sometimes drugs, like alcohol, reduce a user's inhibitions, giving him "permission" to do what he would never otherwise attempt. Several studies have shown that the majority of men who batter women report an alcohol and/or drug problem.[10]

In Greenwich Village, a famous residential section of New York City, Joel Steinberg, a lawyer who regularly used cocaine, murdered his six-year-old adopted daughter, Lisa. When Steinberg gave Lisa the blow that caused her death, Lisa's adoptive mother, Hedda Nussbaum, failed to call an ambulance in time to save her daughter's life. True, Steinberg had abused Hedda Nussbaum for a long time. But like Steinberg, Hedda Nussbaum was a heavy cocaine user.

Drug repeal will not stop tragedies like this from occurring. It could even cause many more.

COMMITTING CRIME TO
PAY FOR DRUGS

As we discussed in chapter 6, drugs cost little to produce; it is the laws against them that inflate their price.

Drug habits are expensive and beyond the reach of most addicts. Because of this, many addicts desperate for their drugs will resort to any means to get them. For drug money, addicts will sell their bodies, deal drugs, steal, even kill. For many, vice and crime are constant companions.

In 1989, a crack-dependent mother was arrested and charged after she sold her eleven-year-old daughter to a rapist for drug money.

To support their heroin habits, a typical New York City addict will steal or otherwise hustle $33,000 a year in cash or goods.[11] To get the $100 to $150 a day for a habit, an addict needs to steal at least $1,000 worth of goods a day.[12] Many addicts steal even more. Altogether, the average drug addict commits three hundred crimes a year.

Much of the property crime in the United States—about 40 percent—is committed by drug abusers looking for cash or goods to support their habits. This translates to four million thefts a year, amounting to $7.5 billion in stolen property (the same amount the federal government proposed spending on the drug war in 1990).[13] How much property crime could be avoided if drugs were affordable?

When they burglarize, some addicts also assault their victims. They beat, rape, and murder them. In his report to the New York County Bar Association, James Ostrowski estimated that more than 1,500 people are murdered each year during such robberies.

DRUG LAW VIOLENCE

Dealers who are violent criminals tend to settle their disputes violently. Observed David Boaz, vice-president of the Cato

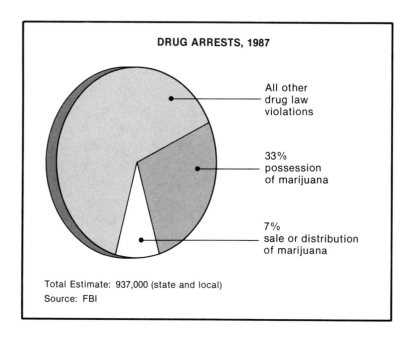

DRUG ARRESTS, 1987

All other
drug law
violations

33%
possession
of marijuana

7%
sale or distribution
of marijuana

Total Estimate: 937,000 (state and local)
Source: FBI

Institute, "You don't see shootouts in the car, liquor, or to-bacco business. But if you have a dispute with another dealer, if he rips you off, you can't sue him, you can't take him to court, you can't do anything except use violence."[14]

Every day in the United States, an average of three people are killed as a result of drug disputes, usually over crack.[15] But innocent victims get caught in the drug dispute cross fires, too.

Just a week after Christmas, Kashaine Green, a twelve-year-old junior high school student, was on her way to visit a friend on Ocean Avenue in Brooklyn, New York. Before she arrived at her friend's home, she was killed in the cross fire of a local drug dispute.

Kashaine had been strolling down the street with Stephen O'Neill, when a friend asked them to step around the corner to exchange a few words of gossip. There Kashaine and Stephen got caught in a spray of Uzi submachine gun bullets. Kashaine, who had dreamed of becoming an artist, died a few hours

88

later. Her friend Stephen suffered a gunshot wound to his mouth. Both were victims of drug crimes, "mushrooms," as drug gunmen refer to the innocent bystanders who pop up unexpectedly in the line of fire.

In 1988, there were more than a hundred victims like Kashaine, even more like Stephen.[16] If drugs were legalized, this kind of violence might come to a halt.

BRIBERY AND CORRUPTION

With so much at stake, drug dealers try to bribe law agents, prosecutors, judges, and parole officers. Human nature being what it is, sometimes they succeed.

Drug laws also contribute to corruption within the system. Occasionally, law enforcement officers, whose job it is to catch drug felons, catch the greed of drug-money fever instead.

Gary P. Callahan was a nineteen-year veteran of the Federal Border Patrol, and was assigned to the Arizona–Mexico border. In 1989, just after midnight, Callahan saw eight to ten backpackers crossing the border. He chased them on foot but was able to catch only one of them. During the chase, however, most of them dropped their backpacks, which were stuffed with cocaine.

According to federal prosecutors, Callahan then hid two of the bags. Later, he delivered them to a prominent Phoenix, Arizona, dentist.

When the dentist admitted to the court that he was a drug smuggler, Callahan was arrested. He lost his career as a law enforcer to the very drugs he was supposed to be confiscating.

A twenty-year veteran of the DEA was also arrested in 1989 on drug-smuggling charges. Along with his two brothers, Edward O'Brien was arrested at Logan International Airport in Boston when he tried to deliver sixty-two pounds of cocaine to an undercover informant. The irony of O'Brien's arrest is that he had helped to close the "French Connection" case in 1973 that broke up a major heroin importation ring.

89

Commented John J. Coleman, Jr., one of O'Brien's friends and head of the Boston DEA office, "Of my hundreds of arrests in my career, this will always be the toughest. Greed," he continued, "can cloud the judgment of the best of us."[17]

Greed clouded the judgment of three former DEA agents charged with laundering more than $608,000 in drug money to Swiss banks. U.S. Attorney Robert Bonner blamed their conduct on the "corrupting effects of drug trafficking." If drugs were legal, this kind of temptation would be removed from law enforcement.

LEGALIZATION MAY DRIVE CRIMINALS OUT OF DRUGS, BUT IT WON'T DRIVE THEM OUT OF CRIME

> *Experience shows that if you go tougher against the narcotics traffickers, they have the capacity to go tougher against you.*
> *—Juan Gabriel Tokatlian, director of international studies at the Univesity of the Andes*

Repeal may drive drug dealers out of business, but it will not necessarily make law-abiding citizens out of them. David Boaz explains: "As conservatives say about guns, if drugs are outlawed, only outlaws will sell drugs."[18]

Some sociologists believe that a segment of the population always finds excitement breaking the law, challenging authority, and defying society's rules. This "culture of crime" is attracted to illicit drugs precisely because they are illegal.

For the same reasons some people are attracted to illegal drugs, they are attracted to crime. Legalizing drugs may keep them out of the drug trade. It may stop their violent drug turf battles. But because they are already drawn to violence and

90

crime, if drugs are legalized, they will probably turn to a new way of earning large sums of money—illegally.

Legalizing drugs will give millions of Americans an opportunity to use drugs—which they already do—without the stigma or fear of breaking the law. It will also abolish the crime of manufacturing or distributing illicit drugs. In addition, it will diminish the temptation among law enforcers to accept bribes and to participate in an illegal market. Finally, it will abolish the crime that comes from fighting over drug turf.

But legalizing drugs cannot change human nature. It cannot improve the social conditions that compel people to engage in crime, nor can it stop people from using drugs as an excuse to be violent. It can't stop the Joel Steinbergs from abusing their families, or the Hedda Nussbaums from neglecting them. It can't even guarantee that the Huwe Burtons will never murder their mothers. In fact, if drugs like crack, PCP, and anabolic steroids were legal, available, and affordable, these crimes might very well increase.

8

DO DRUG LAWS OVERBURDEN ENFORCEMENT?

This is not complicated. It's not complex. It's not
subtle. We need more jails, more prisons, more
courts, more prosecutors. . . . That's just the
plain fact.
                    —William Bennett,
                    Director of National Drug
                    Control Policy

In front of a dilapidated wooden house, rookie cop Edward Byrne of the 103d Precinct in New York City sat alone in his patrol car. Byrne was guarding the home of a witness who was afraid of drug dealers he had reported.

The man's fears were well founded. Four men sought revenge on the witness. Instead, they murdered Officer Byrne.

A year later, DEA agent Everett Hatcher was gunned down on a deserted street on Staten Island, New York. Like Officer Byrne, Hatcher was killed on the job. His job was to enforce the drug laws.

In still another drug war casualty, five lawmen and three National Guardsmen were killed when their helicopter accidentally hit a power line, smashing into the rocky foothills of the Laguna Mountains in California and bursting into flames. The men had been on a nighttime anti-drug smuggling mission, investigating a suspicious-looking parked car.

From 1972 to 1988, the FBI reported that 119 police officers were killed in drug-related incidents, an average of seven a year. More than half of these incidents occurred as police did undercover work or were on drug raids.[1]

Some law enforcers like narcotic squad work because it gives them an exciting break from routine police work. Most, however, find the job tough, dangerous, and often futile. Said one sergeant from the Bronx: "The ones we arrest today, they'll be back on the street in three or four days." Lamented another, "We arrest the same guys, five, six, seven times."

Are shootings like Edward Byrne's or Everett Hatcher's, or the deaths of the eight men killed on the anti-drug mission, too high a price to pay for drug laws?

Should law officers be expected to take such risks to stop drugs that are less risky to use? Is it worth the cost in dollars, manpower, and lives to enforce drug laws? Indeed, *can* drug laws be successfully enforced?

ENFORCING DRUG LAWS IS DIFFICULT

One difficulty in enforcing drug laws is the sheer number of citizens violating them. Arresting one out of every ten citizens using illegal drugs is a difficult, if not impossible, goal. Even if drug law enforcement were limited to cocaine and heroin use, that leaves over six million people to arrest, comparable to the entire population of Chicago.

Another reason drug laws are so difficult to enforce is because of the nature of drug crime. Legal scholars have applied the term "victimless crimes" to drug crimes (and crimes like gambling, prostitution, and loitering). A victimless crime is one in which all the parties involved are guilty. (Victimless does not imply that drug use has no victims—for it does—only that there are no victims in the *legal* sense.)

For example, in burglary, there is a guilty party—the thief. The other party involved—the victim—is likely to report the crime to the police. In contrast, a victimless crime has only guilty parties, none of whom are likely to report the crime.

This leaves police having to rely on witnesses to report drug crimes or on themselves to uncover them.

Unfortunately, many witnesses are too afraid to assist authorities in finding and prosecuting dealers. They are afraid of retribution from the dealers. Worse, they fear that dealers will take revenge on their children.

One housing project resident who was reluctant to report crack dealers in her building or to act as a witness explained why she worried about her twenty-three-year-old son. "He works late at night and has to walk past addicts and pushers to get to our apartment," she told police. "The dealers don't take it out on you," she said. "They take it out on your children."

Another resident admitted knowing of two apartments where crack was sold, information she failed to report to police. She explained that the last time she had, her daughter was attacked, beaten, and threatened with a razor.

Because the majority of drug violations go unreported, police themselves have to find the crimes. As chapter 5 pointed out, they rely on tactics like wiretapping, spying, and searching to ferret out violators. In addition, they hire informants who reveal inside information. Sometimes, too, prosecutors plea bargain with drug felons in exchange for information.

Critics of the drug laws fear that this kind of law enforcement not only erodes some basic civil rights, but increasingly puts law enforcers in a Big Brother role.

It is no longer safe to arrest people simply by knocking on their doors and showing a badge. Today's narcotics detectives are foot soldiers in the trenches, and every raid on a crack house becomes a mini-battle in the war against drugs.

The job of the police is to make cases. They are supposed to arrest suspects and develop evidence against them that can be used by prosecutors. Their job is not to "search and destroy" like soldiers in combat. Yet increasingly, this is what the drug war compels police to do.

It can take months, even years, to arrest a drug dealer or to break up a drug ring. The work is tedious and risky. It requires long hours of vigilance, watching drug dealers come and go, listening to their telephone conversations, even rummaging through their trash before enough evidence can be gathered.

In one typical raid of three apartments where crack was suspected of being dealt, forty armed members of the FBI's SWAT team, as well as local police, were required to batter down the apartment doors, startling its occupants before they had time to get rid of evidence or to defend themselves by reaching for their semiautomatic weapons.

Less complicated, but as dangerous, are the "buy-and-bust" or "sell-and-bust" arrests. In these operations, undercover agents either pose as drug buyers (buy-and-bust) or drug dealers (sell-and-bust). Once a transaction is completed, arrests are made. Then the deal itself is used as evidence.

In order to succeed at this kind of undercover work, agents must win the trust of the people they ultimately intend to arrest. Not all undercover agents are able to, however.

Jerry Ortiz was an undercover agent. After buying drugs from dealers, he would bust them, having gathered enough evidence for their arrest. Officer Ortiz was warned that two of the dealers were planning to rob him. He was determined to proceed with the operation anyway, because he was convinced he had a bond of trust with the dealers.

Ortiz miscalculated. His mistake cost him removal of his spleen, half his liver, and part of his pancreas. For though they may have been unaware of Ortiz's undercover work, the dealers were not trustworthy. Not only did they rob Ortiz, they shot him twice in the back.

Given the increasingly harsh penalties for violating drug laws, guilty parties would sooner kill undercover cops than risk being arrested by them. One young agent who barely survived had half his face blown off trying to arrest a drug dealer during a drug raid.

James Fyfe, a retired New York police officer who once patrolled some of the most dangerous streets in the world, believes the reason so many drug dealers refuse to turn themselves over to police when caught is this: "If you kill a cop, you could conceivably be out of prison in five years. If you get caught possessing large amounts of drugs, you have to do fifteen years in the joint. So if I were a drug dealer and found out I had sold to an undercover, the best thing I could do is blow him away—he can't make the drug case against me, and if he's not alive he probably can't make the murder case against me, either."[2]

INTERDICTION

A large supply of drugs comes from the United States, but an even larger supply enters the country from foreign sources. To get here, the supplies have to cross borders.

Stopping and seizing at the borders drugs that are destined to enter the United States is called interdiction. It has been a major focus of our drug policy. Most interdiction takes place near the borders.

During the 1980s, the federal government concentrated much of its law enforcement effort on interdiction. By 1988, it had spent a billion dollars on it—a third of the annual drug control budget. Given the huge quantities smuggled and the impossibility of sealing the borders completely, interdiction efforts curbed only 10 percent to 20 percent of the drug supply coming into the United States.[3]

One reason for such dismal statistics is the drug runners' cunning; they easily stay ahead of law enforcement efforts.

Max Mermelstein, a former drug dealer connected to the Medellín cartel, explained how adept traffickers have become at finding holes in the government's drug nets. "Basically, the way the cartel has been able to exist and flourish," he told federal officials, "is they can change faster than the United States government can."[4]

Mermelstein illustrated his point with the following example. From 1981 to 1985, the Medellín cartel kept a twenty-four-hour radio watch on United States law enforcement channels.

Whenever a federal authority switched to a different channel, cartel monitors would sweep the radio bands until they found the new channel. Once they had identified it, they could determine where federal planes and ships were. Then they could avoid them and fly their cartel planes laden with illegal cargo, catching the federal agents off guard.

The cartel refused to take any chances. "If we didn't have the frequency," said Mermelstein, "we didn't fly."

SEALING THE BORDERS

Is it realistic to expect to be able to keep illegal drugs from crossing the borders when there are over five thousand miles of undefended border with Canada, almost two thousand with Mexico, and when so much of the border area is sparsely populated wilderness or desert?

Added to those land borders are the thousands of miles of coastline, six hundred miles in Florida alone, also impossible to seal off.

The task of patrolling the borders is delegated primarily to the U.S. Customs Agency. It is assisted by the FBI, the DEA, and the U.S. Coast Guard.

Even with a billion-dollar budget, there is never enough personnel to adequately patrol the borders. Consider what they are up against: In 1988, 355,000,000 people, 100,000 vehicles, 220,000 vessels, 635,000 aircraft, and 8,000,000 containers entered or reentered the country.[5]

Customs officials estimate that they search only 5 percent of the vehicles or people and only 3 percent of the containers passing through their points of entry.[6] To search more poses several problems. First, it would make it too hard to keep up the free flow of commerce and tourism; searching more people would create intolerably long delays at the entry ports. Second, since most people going through customs are innocent, such searching would be a serious infringement on their rights.

Even when the Coast Guard searches crafts they are tipped

off about, their effort yields drugs only once in eight searches. Moreover, it is impossible to survey all boats. Southern Florida alone has more than 120,000 registered pleasure boats. While the Coast Guard has interdicted record amounts of drugs in recent years, it remains a fraction of what enters through coastal waters.

Airborne interdiction faces many of the same problems as ground and sea interdiction. The results aren't any better. Although 55,000 pounds of cocaine were confiscated from private aircraft in 1987, for example, it was minuscule compared with what entered the country during that one year.[7]

Regardless of the excellent equipment used to detect illegal aircraft, as Mermelstein pointed out to federal authorities, many go undetected. Even if officials could detect every suspicious aircraft, they can't force each one down for inspection. And that's not considering the fact that they'd also be forcing down innocent passengers.

Drug-running pilots find many ways to elude arrest. When law enforcement officials began catching them at drop-off points in Georgia and Florida, for example, pilots switched to aircraft that could fly long-range missions. That way they simply dropped their cargo and headed back to home base, without ever landing their aircraft. When southern Florida enforcement was beefed up against Latin American drug running, smugglers switched their drop-offs to remote beaches in Long Island and other Northeast coastal spots.

Pilots and their backers have invested in more elaborate equipment, such as million-dollar turboprops equipped with extra fuel tanks and advanced electronics. Such improvements allow them to increase their flight range and improve their success rates.

Once drugs enter the United States, law enforcement agencies are faced with another challenge: stopping the distribution to cities and towns across America. Although some drug running is done by aircraft, most is done by car or truck.

Like international drug runs, illegal domestic cargoes are cleverly disguised. For example, shipments have been concealed in trailers containing smelly fish, sewn into stuffed toy animals, and hidden in fuel tanks and mufflers. Unless drug enforcers were to stop every single vehicle traveling U.S. highways and roads, they could never begin to catch most of the illegal drug traffic.

Larry Orton, a special Drug Enforcement Administration agent in El Paso, Texas, advises that interdiction is not an answer to the drug problem. "There are more ways to bring the drugs into the country," he says, "than we have the ability or wherewithal to stop. You can't just go willy-nilly stopping people in the country."[8]

ERADICATION

Although most illegal drug crops are grown in foreign countries, about 20 percent to 25 percent of the marijuana Americans consume is grown here. Seven states—California, Hawaii, Kansas, Louisiana, Tennessee, Kentucky, and Missouri—are the largest producers.

Law enforcement agencies are faced with the problem of destroying these crops and arresting the people cultivating them. In 1987, the DEA eradicated (destroyed) approximately 7.4 million cannabis plants.

For marijuana producers, the stakes are high, the profits even higher. None want to see their crops destroyed. Faced with harsher sentences, they try hard to avoid arrest.

Some resourceful growers set up booby traps to keep law enforcement agents off their property. One ploy is to conceal razors strung between tree limbs at eye level. Then, as agents walk through the woods on their way to arrest producers, they unexpectedly encounter the razors.

Another ploy is to set up land mines on the property that explode when agents accidentally step on them.

As a crop, marijuana is similar to tobacco. Given that tobacco kills 350,000 people a year and is far more addictive, can we justify arresting marijuana producers while legally subsidizing tobacco farmers?

MILITARY INVOLVEMENT

The military already participates in the drug war via the U.S. Coast Guard. In addition, it has helped several foreign nations to carry out eradication programs. One of the most elaborate military operations occurred in Panama in 1989. There, twenty thousand American troops invaded Panama to flush out General Manuel Antonio Noriega, charged with drug dealing.

In 1986, in an operation called Blast Furnace, Army pilots in U.S. Army helicopters transported Bolivian forces on raids against drug-manufacturing sites in the Bolivian jungle.

Several congressional leaders are requesting that even more military support be enlisted in the war against drugs. Due to changes in drug policy, along with a change in attitude at the Pentagon, the U.S. military is preparing to take an even larger role in the drug war. For example, as this book goes to press, there is discussion about sending military advisors to Colombia to assist that government's struggle against drugs.

In 1988, Congress legislated $300 million in military funds, which were targeted specifically to drug enforcement. The following year, it increased that figure to $470 million.[9] Even more funds were targeted for subsequent years.

Drug laws are difficult, maybe impossible, to enforce. Yet are we ready to become a nation where military personnel are needed to enforce our laws?

BURDEN ON COURTS
AND PRISONS

> We've taken a person off the street who is a junkie and we've made him a felon. What have we accomplished? We've jammed our system and we haven't solved the drug problem.
> —Martin Murphy, Legal Aid
> Society lawyer

100

```
                    TOTAL DRUG ARRESTS
           1983:        666,000
           1984:        708,000
           1985:        811,000
           1986:        824,000
           1987:        937,000
           1988:      1,100,000

  Source: FBI
```

Nationwide, about half the prisoners in federal custody are drug offenders. And, according to Attorney General Richard Thornburgh, "There is no end in sight."

In 1988, there were over a million drug arrests in the United States. This represented a 65 percent increase in just five years. Together an increase in drug crimes and tougher law enforcement were responsible for that increase.

The problem with so many arrests is that neither the courts nor the prisons can keep pace. And because they can't, the message on the streets is this: We'll arrest you, but don't worry; we can't handle your case in court and we don't have room to lock you up for long.

```
              PRISON POPULATION INCREASE

                        1980              1988
           State:     282,398           535,009
           Federal:    20,562           433,134

  Source: U.S. Department of Justice
```

Many jails and prisons are operating at 100 percent capacity. In the Harris County Jail in Houston, the nation's second-

101

largest county jail, half the inmates are incarcerated on drug-related charges. Altogether there are 8,200 inmates, which is twice the jail's capacity.

Conditions in many prisons are deplorable. Prisoners are doubled up in cells. Many have to sleep on floors and in day rooms. It is so bad, in fact, that some of the inmates have filed lawsuits claiming that the conditions violate their constitutional rights. In addition, jails don't take drugs away—it's just as easy to get drugs in jail as on the street.

ESTIMATED FEDERAL DRUG SEIZURES
(in pounds)

	FY 1987	FY 1988	Change
Cocaine	140,000	198,000	+29%
Heroin	1,400	2,150	+35%
Marijuana	2,000,000	1,660,000	−17%

Source: Based on data provided by U.S. Coast Guard, U.S. Customs Service, Drug Enforcement Administration, Federal Bureau of Investigation, and INS/Border Patrol (limited reporting). Figures do not include drug seizures in foreign jurisdictions.

To meet the need for more prisons, during the 1980s the government doubled the number of cells. This still left an acute shortage, however. According to the Department of Justice, overcoming it requires that 800 to 1,000 new beds be added *per week.*[10]

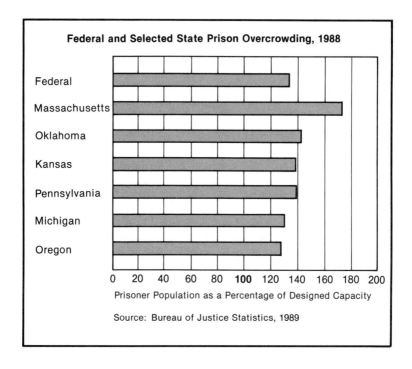

Federal and Selected State Prison Overcrowding, 1988

Prisoner Population as a Percentage of Designed Capacity

Source: Bureau of Justice Statistics, 1989

Because of the shortage, many prisoners are released early. In Texas, for example, prisoners are serving only one month for every twelve months of their sentence (then they are released on parole). Where overcrowding is acute, they may serve none of their sentence locked up; instead, they are placed on parole the entire time.

Drug laws have also created a new prison population, crack-dependent pregnant women.

As chapter 5 discussed, crack is a serious problem among pregnant women, especially in the inner cities. Despite the willingness and desire many women express to enter treatment programs, there is a dearth of programs that will accept them. Yet there is a growing trend to arrest, convict, and jail these women in order to get them off crack before they give birth.

Critics suggest that the drug policy ought to reevaluate this practice. They question whether jailing these women instead of offering them treatment is a decent social policy.

THE LOAD ON THE COURTS

The courts are as overburdened as the prisons. There aren't nearly enough prosecutors, judges, courtrooms, laboratories, and grand juries to handle the increase in drug arrests.

The shortage is particularly bad in cities like New York. The Tactical Narcotics Teams (TNT) of the New York Police Department have saturated drug-infested neighborhoods and made thousands of arrests. The arrests, in turn, have swamped the already overloaded judicial system. Some New York City prosecutors are assigned to as many as 150 cases; some criminal court judges as many as 400.

The courthouses themselves are overcrowded. One judge described a situation in which two courtrooms were divided by only a few filing cabinets. The two juries were backed up against the cabinets. The judge called the situation a disgrace.

Other judges think it is more than a disgrace. Comments Judge Ivar Goldart, deputy attorney in charge of the New York Legal Aid Society's criminal defense division, "The overcrowding is a far cry from that which we describe as justice."[11]

One reason drug cases place such a burden on the judicial system is because they are so massive and complex; a typical case takes several months in court.

In addition, the backlog of cases causes a serious delay. In turn, this delay costs taxpayers thousands more dollars than if arraignments and trials could be set sooner. It also imposes a serious infringement on defendants' rights to speedy trials.

The judicial overload compels prosecutors to do more plea bargaining in order to avoid lengthy trials. Plea bargaining is the negotiation between the prosecutor and the defendant whereby the defendant pleads guilty to a lesser charge. The defendant then receives a lighter sentence than if he or she had gone to trial and been convicted on the original charge.

104

For example, whereas a defendant might have received a twenty-five-year prison sentence if convicted of the original charge, after plea bargaining, he or she might receive only probation or a few months in jail.

Not all defendants go for plea bargaining. It may offer them a lighter sentence, but the sentence may still be too harsh. Also, by pleading guilty to a lesser charge, the defendant relinquishes his or her chance to be acquitted (found innocent). As a result, more and more defendants are taking a chance on trials. They are also increasing their demand for appeals on previous trials. All this strains the system even further.

If marijuana were legalized nationwide, the number of drug arrests could be cut by at least one-third. Another way to ease the burden on the criminal justice system would be to offer treatment on demand to drug abusers instead of arresting or incarcerating them. First-time addicts could be offered the option of a six-month treatment program. Those arrested for possession of small amounts of drugs could be required to attend out-patient programs like group counseling. Such approaches not only take much of the load off the judicial system, but they also improve the drug users' chances of staying out of the system in the future.

As we learned in the previous chapter, drug use contributes to family violence. In New York City, for example, crack contributed to a tripling of cases in which parents abused or neglected their children. In fact, three-fourths of the juvenile deaths resulting from abuse or neglect in 1987 were caused by parents who were abusing drugs.[12]

These domestic cases frequently wind up in court. So, although legalizing drugs is bound to ease the burden in criminal court, it would probably increase that on family courts. In addition, juvenile courts may also experience an increase, since more juveniles might use drugs that would remain illegal for minors to use.

Judging by their recent records, law enforcement agencies are more effective than ever at making drug arrests, destroying illegal crops, and seizing illegal drugs. Still, crack use has escalated and drug violence has increased. And the courts and prisons have had trouble keeping up.

It is probably possible to enforce drug laws, but it will take billions of dollars and a huge commitment. We will end up with over a million inmates in jail, and millions more out on probation. We will risk becoming a police state if the National Guard and other militia are drafted to help win the war.

Legalizing drugs is not our only alternative. Currently 70 percent of the drug control budget goes to law enforcement and only 30 percent to treatment and prevention.[13] Why not reverse the ratio? Why not spend even more on the other social problems that compel people to use drugs in the first place, or to earn money from selling them?

In the meantime, we have not yet reached Armageddon. Law enforcers are doing their best to win the war on drugs; many are risking their lives for it. No matter how overloaded it is, the justice system is functioning. As one judge pointed out, "It still works. Courts remain open. Cases are being processed." The question remains, however: What can we do to make it better?

9

THE EFFECT OF LEGALIZATION ON FOREIGN POLICY

There are probably few issues which have caused greater strains in our relations with other nations, particularly with our Latin American neighbors, than that of international drug trafficking.

> —Senate Report on Drugs, Law Enforcement, and Foreign Policy

A mile high, in the Andean mountain city of Medellín, Colombia, reside the most successful criminals in history. These Latin American billionaires, known as the Medellín cartel, are said to be responsible for 80 percent of the illegal cocaine and crack sold in the United States. Each year they export between 300 and 400 metric tons of cocaine, which may add as much as $4 billion to their coffers.[1]

They also generate violence and corruption. Since 1981, the cartel has murdered in Colombia 50 judges, including half the Supreme Court justices, 170 judicial employees, a leading presidential candidate, two ministers of justice, a head of the National Police Anti-Narcotics Bureau, an attorney general, a dozen journalists, a leading newspaper editor, and more than 400 police and military personnel.

When they kill, they kill mercilessly. They have hung

victims from trees and disemboweled them. They shot Colonel Jaime Ramierez Gomez, head of a national narcotics command, twenty-eight times in front of his wife and children. And in 1989 at a political rally in Bogotá, in full view of 10,000 people, a hit team opened fire on Senator Luis Carlos Galan.

The cartel's corruption is as widespread as its terror. Reports are that half of Colombia's congressional seats are filled by politicians whose campaigns were funded by the cartel. Some regions are so corrupt that the drug cartels literally support government officials. One former police officer explained how colleagues were receiving $128 in wages from the government and $225 in monthly bribes from the cartel, while captains received $180 from the government and $5,000 in bribes.[2]

Although the Medellín cartel has captured the foreign spotlight in the drug war, there is a chorus of involvement by other nations. The Sicilian Mafia, for one, has taken over in Europe where the French Connection left off.

Illegal drug trafficking is truly a global affair. Its tentacles reach over oceans and seas, through skies, and across borders. What began as a struggle between a few nations like China and England grew to an international beast of crime, greed, and corruption. According to a 1988 report by the U.S. State Department, over forty-eight nations are involved in drug trafficking, either supplying or transporting drugs.[3]

With so many nations producing and transporting illegal drugs, the drug war cannot be confined to United States territory. Wherever drugs are cultivated, processed, and shipped, and their profits laundered, is battle turf.

Given the international scope of the drug war, how would legalization affect foreign policy? Would it improve it? Or would it breach international treaties and weaken our resolve to end drug use?

Can legalization drive organizations like the Medellín cartel and the Mafia out of the drug business? Or will they become our legitimate business partners because of it?

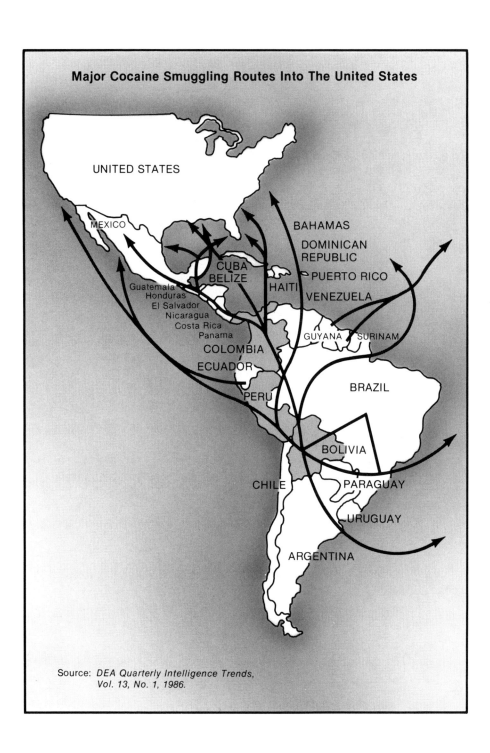

Major Cocaine Smuggling Routes Into The United States

UNITED STATES

MEXICO

BAHAMAS

DOMINICAN
REPUBLIC

CUBA
BELIZE

PUERTO RICO

Guatemala
Honduras
El Salvador
Nicaragua
Costa Rica
Panama

HAITI

VENEZUELA

GUYANA   SURINAM

COLOMBIA

ECUADOR

BRAZIL

PERU

BOLIVIA

CHILE

PARAGUAY

URUGUAY

ARGENTINA

Source: *DEA Quarterly Intelligence Trends,*
Vol. 13, No. 1, 1986.

INTERNATIONAL TREATIES

As the history of drug laws indicates, the goal of the first international treaty—the 1912 Hague Convention—was to "gradually suppress the nonmedical use of drugs."[4] In the decades that followed those first efforts came additional treaties, each in response to a new concern about drug use.

Then, in 1961, all of the treaties were consolidated. The combined treaty, the Single Convention on Narcotic Drugs, was signed by sixty-four nations. Since 1961, the Single Convention has been amended and the number of nations signing it has doubled. One of the primary goals of the Single Convention was to limit the worldwide production of drugs to what was needed for scientific and medical use.

A year after the Single Convention, a second international treaty was executed, the Psychotropic Convention of 1971. The purpose of this treaty was to establish international control of amphetamines, barbiturates, and hallucinogens.

Finally, on December 20, 1988, after four years of negotiations, forty-three nations signed the most recent United Nations treaty, the Vienna Convention. Its primary focus is on drug trafficking, including issues like money laundering and extradition.

In addition to the U.N. treaties, the United States has worked out agreements and treaties with individual nations concerning drug control.

EXTRADITION

An important aspect of international drug control is extradition, the surrendering of a suspect to another jurisdiction or country for prosecution. It is essential to law enforcement because it ensures that illegal drug producers and traffickers are brought to justice.

Extradition is mutual. We can extradite drug dealers out of the country as well as ask that they be extradited to us.

110

At present, the United States has extradition treaties with over 100 countries,[5] but many have no provisions for drug charges. Other treaties do, but the governments involved refuse to cooperate. One reason is that the 1988 U.S. Drug Act allows for the death penalty; some governments have been reluctant to surrender citizens who could receive that penalty.

Extradition is the leading fear of the Medellín cartel. In 1979 Colombia and the United States signed an extradition treaty. Then in 1984, Colombia extradited sixteen people, including Carlos Lehder Rivas, a leader of the Medellín cartel. In retaliation, the cartel stormed the Colombian federal courthouse, murdering half the Supreme Court and killing over 100 court employees. Yielding to such pressure, the Supreme Court declared the treaty unconstitutional in 1987.

There were no more extraditions until 1989. When presidential candidate Luis Carlos Galan was assassinated, the Colombian government turned once again to extradition as a tool in the drug war. And once more the cartel threatened to retaliate.

Through an organization called the "Extraditables," the cartel delivered a bouquet to a judge in Cali, Colombia. On it was a message promising to murder ten judges for each Colombian extradited.

Extradition agreements are ineffective if a nation cannot or will not respect the treaty. For instance, we have an extradition treaty with Pakistan. Yet since 1984, the Pakistani government has failed repeatedly to extradite an individual who was charged in the U.S. with drug dealing.

Other nations to which the U.S. has extradited known drug dealers are so corrupt that their courts either free the dealers or give them extremely lenient sentences.

Because domestic law takes precedence over international law, the United States is at liberty to legalize drugs regardless of treaties. To do so, however, would breach the agreements. It would also seriously detract from our commitment to stop international drug trafficking.

INTERNATIONAL COOPERATION

Many nations refuse to cooperate in international drug control. Iran, for example, is a major producer of opium and heroin. But ever since the Shah's fall from power and the 1979 U.S. Embassy takeover by Iranian terrorists, U.S. diplomatic relations with Iran have been severed. This leaves the United States with no influence on Iranian drug trafficking except through interdiction of exports.

Some nations officially agree to cooperate, but corruption is so widespread among their officials and law enforcement agencies that it is exceedingly difficult for them to cooperate. Some regions are so corrupt, in fact, that drug lords virtually hold the government under siege, controlling many officials.

John Lawn, the DEA administrator, testified that in Colombia "individuals, especially judges, who cannot be corrupted are given the option of silver or lead—take the money or be killed. Even good individuals in that environment," he acknowledged, "find themselves corrupted."[6]

Occasionally a nation with a history of uncooperation will change its diplomatic course. Ever since Fidel Castro came to power over thirty years ago, for example, the U.S. has had no diplomatic relations with Cuba.

In recent years, as federal agencies effectively closed off airspace over the Bahamas, drug-running pilots from Colombia sought airspace over Cuba, which lay directly on their route to Florida. Corrupt Cuban officials tolerated these unauthorized overflights. Some were even bribed to allow pilots to refuel and service their aircraft. Other pilots dropped their contraband cargo onto boats waiting in Cuba's territorial waters. During the first half of 1989, thirty-nine such drop-offs were spotted by the DEA.[7]

Although Castro tried to rid his country of the scourge of drugs, he never cooperated with this country in its efforts to do the same. But in June 1989, Cuba made a surprising turnaround.

After learning that fourteen of his top officials were in-

112

volved with the Medellín cartel, Castro condemned the illegal drug running. On July 9, 1989, he delivered a speech in which he offered to cooperate with the U.S. "Cuba and the United States really have to discuss how to manage such things," he said, "and arrange to form communication in this common battle."

Then, perhaps to demonstrate his earnestness, Castro ordered the swift execution of four of the arrested officials. Among them was General Arnaldo Ochoa Sanchez, former commander in chief of Cuban troops in Angola and a national hero.

In 1986, the Anti-Drug Abuse Act gave the U.S. government some leverage to deal with uncooperative nations. It amended the Foreign Assistance Act of 1961 to allow the U.S. to withhold up to half the financial assistance it had promised to those nations. Loans of funds for development may also be restricted. These sanctions have seldom been exercised, for, if he deems that vital national interests are at stake, the president can ignore the sanction and certify the country.

U.S. PRESENCE IN FOREIGN NATIONS

The original drug laws were limited to the United States. Following World War II, efforts were expanded when the first foreign office of the DEA was opened in Rome. Today the DEA has nearly 300 agents stationed in more than forty countries.

The State Department also plays a vital role in international drug control. It has narcotics assistance units in thirteen major drug source and transit countries, and in 1987 it assisted more than forty foreign governments with drug control.

One other U.S. government agency with an important part in drug control is the Agency for International Development (AID). One of AID's major agendas is to help farmers find alternatives to growing illegal crops.

Foreign governments may welcome the presence of U.S.

narcotics agents, especially when they have a shortage of resources. However, not all their citizens do.

Much of our narcotics work consists of intelligence gathering. Explaining her resentment of the presence of U.S. narcotics agents, one Latin American critic voiced this comparison: "How would U.S. citizens feel about the KGB knocking on their doors, asking them questions or searching their homes?"

Another cause of resentment is our double standard. Occasionally DEA agents will do in other countries what may be prohibited here.

One instance occurred in 1989 in Mexico. DEA agents suspected Rene Martin Verdugo-Urquidez of drug smuggling. Together with Mexican police, agents searched his two homes—without a search warrant.

In the U.S. Supreme Court appeal of the case, the Justice Department planned to argue that search warrants outside the United States are impractical. "In any event," a spokesperson for the court said, "the right against unreasonable searches and seizures does not extend to all persons throughout the world."[8]

ERADICATION

An essential part of U.S. foreign narcotics control is to help governments destroy illegal crops before they can be harvested. Eradication is done in two ways: either by manually digging up the plants or by aerially spraying herbicides.

Manual eradication is time consuming. Even so, five ten-man teams in Brazil literally pulled out five million illegal plants in one year.

In contrast, aerial spraying is far more efficient. Hundreds of acres can be sprayed in the time it takes a team of men to eradicate one acre.

Aerial eradication has a serious drawback, however. Some of the chemicals used are toxic, increasing the risk of cancer or birth defects. Others can cause serious damage to the ecological system.

114

One of the most frequently used chemicals is a U.S.-made herbicide known as Spike. U.S. narcotics officials tried to reassure Peru's public that Spike is harmless. "It is less toxic than aspirin, nicotine, and nitrate fertilizers," said Ann B. Wrobleski, a government spokesperson.

Environmental advocates sharply disagree. They believe that at best Spike is a gamble, particularly in the fragile rain forest environments where Peruvian coca is grown. Moreover, Spike sold in the United States carries a label warning that it kills trees, shrubs, and other forms of desirable vegetation and should be kept out of lakes, ponds, and streams.

Eradication is not the only threat to the environment. Coca growers do their share of damage. In Peru they have destroyed over half a million acres of tropical rain forest.[9] But drug laws contribute to the damage as well. If drugs were legal, there would be no reason to damage the environment with potentially dangerous chemicals. (Of course, this might be offset by an increase in drug production, which would put more land under drug cultivation.)

EFFECT ON FOREIGN ECONOMIES

Experts predict that worldwide, the illegal drug market generates $500 billion (twice the amount of U.S. currency in circulation). The effect legalization would have on the world economy is less predictable.

As with any product in a free marketplace, if there is a demand for it, there will be people willing to meet the demand. Profits and employment from drugs would continue. Without the crime tariff, however, they would probably not continue at their current excess.

Hundreds of thousands of otherwise poor farmers depend on illegal crops for their livelihood. In Bolivia alone, experts estimate that the drug industry provides work for 300,000 people. If drugs were legal and the demand for them remained—or even rose—these people would not be out of work. They would also no longer need to be concerned with losing their crops to eradication or property seizures. However, they would be earning a lot less money. For many, what they now earn is not enough to raise them above poverty.

On the other hand, foreigners whose main crop is cannabis may find themselves looking for alternatives.

Mark Kleinman of Harvard's Kennedy School of Government conducted an excellent study of the illegal marijuana market. He found that several years ago tighter controls at the border had reduced marijuana imports. This reduction stimulated an American marijuana industry. It also gave rise to a more potent form of marijuana—sinsemilla.

In four years, the American market produced one-fourth the marijuana sold in the United States. It was also the most potent marijuana in the world.

Low-grade marijuana normally has a tetrahydrocannabinol (THC) content of 1 percent to 2 percent. In contrast, some American marijuana has reached THC levels as high as 18 percent. This increase prompted one observer to draw a comparison to alcohol. "It's like a fellow looking for a beer and winding up with a triple martini."[10]

Certainly if marijuana were legalized, Americans might easily dominate the worldwide market for it, pushing aside foreign importers.

CONFLICT OF INTERESTS

From 1987 to 1989, a Senate subcommittee, headed by Senator John Kerry, investigated the problem of international narcotics trafficking. Among the findings reported were incidents where the U.S. State Department had put its agenda ahead of foreign drug control.

For example, in 1986, the State Department supported the contras, who were trying to overthrow Nicaragua's Sandinista government. The department believed it was in the U.S.'s best interest to support the rebels. Part of that support included a $800,000 payment to four companies distributing humanitarian aid to the contras. The State Department did this despite the knowledge that the companies were owned and operated by narcotics traffickers.

116

Another conflict arose in Panama. Populist leader General Omar Torrijos tried to develop Panama as an international banking center. He did this by eliminating the income tax and by developing strict bank secrecy laws like the Swiss have. As a result, Panama did become an international banking center— and a major money-laundering one.

The United States was aware of allegations of what was occurring in Panama's banking community, but because it was negotiating transfer of the Panama Canal, it befriended Torrijos and even trained 15,000 of his troops. Basically, the State Department had turned a blind eye to the money laundering.

Its eyes stayed closed when the United States allied itself with another Panamanian, General Manuel Antonio Noriega. General Noriega was sly enough to manipulate both the DEA and the State Department. And, while he was befriended by both agencies, he earned between $200 million and $300 million by accepting bribes to protect illegal drug traffickers and their interests. The State Department received many reports on Noriega's drug activities, but not until the *New York Times* ran an exposé of Noriega did the department stop feigning ignorance.

Only as recently as 1989 has U.S. drug policy ranked higher than other Latin American affairs. Legalization would reorganize national priorities; drug control would revert to being an internal problem, not a part of foreign policy. Instead of trying to enforce drug control in other countries, our attention would be directed to reducing the demand for drugs here through treatment and prevention.

PUSH DOWN, POP UP

Trying to control the international narcotics supply is like trying to ride a seesaw. When one country "pushes down" its supply, there is always another to "pop up" and take its place.

Early in the 1960s, Turkey grew most of the opium for the heroin smuggled into the United States. (The opium was actually grown in Turkey but processed in France.) When this "French Connection" was busted in 1973, the Turkish gov-

117

ernment cooperated with the United States and France to eradicate most of Turkey's illicit opium crop. In large part, it was successful.

Unfortunately, when the Turkish supply was "pushed down," a new supply "popped up" in Mexico. In response, the United States pressured Mexico. Success there reduced Mexican heroin imports from nearly 90 percent of the U.S. supply to only a third of it. Another "push down" for foreign narcotics control.

And the new pop up? The Golden Triangle (Burma–Thailand–Laos) supplying heroin and later the Golden Crescent (Afghanistan–Pakistan–Iran) supplying opium.

Legalization would make U.S. foreign drug policy obsolete. It could incur the wrath of nations who feel betrayed by it. It also could drive drug cartels and other criminals out of the U.S. market.

If the United States continued to get drugs from foreign sources, it could suddenly find itself in business with the very criminal organizations it abhors. Since those organizations are already so wealthy, powerful, and entrenched in their own governments' politics, their presence would be a continuing menace.

Legalization also will not feed the Andean peasants who earned less than $10 a year before growing coca plants. Legalization or not, corruption, violence, and poverty are issues with which the world has to deal.

As long as nations refuse or are too politically corrupt to cooperate, putting an end to international drug trafficking is hopeless. We have already begun two wars against drugs. To wage a real war with troops, guns, tanks, and bombs is unimaginable. Given the hilly terrain where drugs are grown, as well as the cunning savagery of drug traffickers, fighting a war with forty-eight nations would dwarf our failure in Vietnam. And the push down–pop up cycle shows that any victory would be short-lived.

10

WHAT'S THE GAMBLE?

It is unlikely that humanity at large will ever be able to dispense with artificial paradises.
—Aldous Huxley

Drug laws touch upon many issues, from crime and justice to economics and foreign policy. This is why legalizing them is not a black-or-white, right-or-wrong decision. It is complicated. And so the odds for its success or failure are difficult to call.

Legalizing drugs is a social gamble, a huge one if all drugs were legalized. Regardless, some people want to take the risk. They ask, "What if?"

What if drugs were legalized? Would more people try them? Would more people use them regularly? Would more people abuse them?

Will treatment be available? How many users will be convinced to seek it? How much will it cost and who will pay for it?

If drug use were legal, how would we convince people that drugs were not okay to use?

Finally, if legalization doesn't work, if the outcome is catastrophic, could we rewind the clock? Or will it be too late?

LAWS KEEP PEOPLE
FROM USING DRUGS

For over seventy-five years, we have had laws against drugs. More laws and tougher laws. Yet Americans persist in using drugs. In the early 1960s, only one out of every fifty Americans had tried an illicit drug.[1] Now, three decades later, one out of every three has. We can only wonder how many more might have tried drugs if they were legal.

When alcohol was prohibited, the number of Americans who took a drink decreased considerably. Then, when the Volstead Act legalized it once again, more Americans started drinking. In fact, with no laws banning alcohol, the number of drinkers doubled within a short while.

For many of the same reasons laws kept people from drinking, laws keep people from using drugs. Therefore, repealing drug laws could produce the same result that repealing the Volstead Act did and could result in more drug use than before.

In a 1986 survey of New Jersey high school students, 70 percent of the students who did not use drugs said it was because there were laws against them.[2] If the laws were repealed, would they and others like them be more likely to use drugs? Moreover, how do drug laws stop Americans from using drugs?

For some people, laws keep them lawful; it is their desire to be law-abiding citizens. They respect laws too much to break them.

For others, it is the fear of getting arrested and imprisoned that keeps them from abusing drugs. In 1986, three-fourths of the people convicted of drug violation charges were sentenced to an average prison term of more than five years. Even if possession of drugs resulted in only a fine, the risk is not worth it for most people.

For still others, drug laws keep them from using drugs because of the message: If there is a law proscribing drug use, then using drugs must be wrong.

As we have learned in previous chapters, drug laws add to the price of illicit drugs, keeping them rather costly. The 1989 National Drug Control Strategy Report estimated that legalization would lower the price of cocaine to a mere 5 percent of its current selling price. This means that instead of $60 to $80 a gram, cocaine would cost $3 to $4. Even if a gram of cocaine sold for $10 (the highest amount that could destroy the black market), an average dose would be only 50 cents. "An amount," the report noted, "that is well within the lunch-money budget of the average American elementary school student."[3]

The cost of marijuana would also plummet; three joints could be as low as a dollar—again, within the reach of even young children.[4]

Some people avoid drugs because they don't know where to buy them. Others are afraid to go to the places where drugs are sold. Still others are reluctant to deal with the kind of people who sell drugs. In those ways, drug laws keep people away from drugs. Thus, by permitting honest people to sell drugs in convenient locations, legalization would remove those barriers.

LEGALIZATION WOULD MAKE DRUGS SAFER TO USE

With the end of alcohol prohibition came the beginning of government regulation and quality control of liquor. No longer did consumers have to fear that their drinks were unsafe or even deadly. If drugs were legalized, the same regulation and quality control could be applied to them. As a result, people who avoid drugs because they don't know exactly what is in them might be more inclined to buy and use them, knowing the products' ingredients.

For instance, in order to stretch their profits, dealers often "cut" drugs with substances like arsenic and strychnine. These substances can cause severe complications, even death.

Buying drugs on the street keeps users ignorant of a drug's

real potency. This can be dangerous and is the cause of most drug overdoses.

In 1981, the Model Drug Paraphernalia Act banned the sale of water pipes, bongs, and other apparatus used to smoke marijuana and hashish. Because most of the carcinogens (cancer-causing substances) in hashish and marijuana are water soluble, the paraphernalia allowed water to absorb the carcinogens in the smoke. This made the drugs less harmful. Thus, legalizing marijuana and subsequently repealing the act would give users access to safer apparatus.

Drug laws make it difficult for intravenous drug users to get sterile needles that could curb the transmission of AIDS (though such difficulty may deter others from shooting drugs into their veins with unsterile needles). A fourth of all AIDS victims are intravenous drug users who probably caught the disease from contaminated needles, which addicts often share. In large cities like New York and Los Angeles, half of all the intravenous drug users are infected with the AIDS virus.

Intravenous drug users are not the only drug-related victims of AIDS. Each year, thousands of babies are born to mothers who infected them during pregnancy or nursing. In addition, 70 percent of new heterosexual AIDS cases are due to contact with AIDS-infected IV drug users.

Today, alcohol and tobacco consumers know exactly what they are purchasing. If drugs were legal, drug users would also be informed consumers. Regulation and quality control would stop drug "cutting," would inform buyers of a drug's potency, and would make drug paraphernalia and sterile needles available. With those improvements, drug users could avoid many of the dangers they now face.

SELLING TO MINORS

Minors are not permitted to purchase alcohol or tobacco. If drugs were legalized, they probably would not be permitted to purchase drugs. Yet even now, while drugs are controlled, it is largely minors who use them. Minors account for three-fourths of all drug use; the average age of first-time users is only thirteen years.

Experience teaches that when a substance is legal for adults, young people will use it, too. For example, more than 90 percent of all high school seniors have tried alcohol; more than two-thirds have tried cigarettes. Both are legal. In contrast, only half have tried marijuana, 15 percent cocaine, and less than 1 percent heroin.[5]

In Alaska, it is legal to possess four ounces of marijuana for personal use at home. (Four ounces equals 120 joints.) In a national survey of junior and senior high school students, only about a fourth of those responding had tried marijuana. Yet a survey of only Alaskan students revealed that twice as many students—one-half—had tried marijuana.[6]

LEGALIZATION REMOVES THE TEMPTATION TO RECRUIT NEW DRUG USERS

Most people did not buy the first drugs they used. Rather, they were "turned on," or given the drugs, by friends or people they knew. Many times these were people selling drugs to support their own habit; they were looking for new customers who could ensure a steady income for them. John Kaplan, author of *The Hardest Drug: Heroin and Public Policy,* found that the average heroin seller is supported by three heavy users.

Legalization might take away the junkie's incentive to recruit new users. But does it take away the supplier's desire to find new ones?

The possibility always exists that drug users will recruit people, even if they don't want to sell them drugs. In fact, this is why the federal drug control strategy targets the casual or regular drug user, and not necessarily the hard-core addict. In the opinion of the writers of the National Drug Control Strategy report, casual users are highly contagious. "Regular users," the report noted, "are likely to have intact families, social lives and jobs. They are likely to 'enjoy' drugs for the pleasure they offer. Therefore, they are more willing and able to proselytize drug use—by action or example—among people they know."[7]

Personal recruitment is not the only way to lure new people into drug use. After all, what is there to stop a free market drug industry from luring new users through advertisements or other marketing campaigns?

ADDICTION COULD DECREASE

Some experts, perhaps out on a limb, argue that legalizing drugs would give society a chance to accustom itself to dangerous drugs. While there might be more drug use since use would not be taboo, there might also be less drug abuse.

Although marijuana does not produce the same kind of dependence as heroin or cocaine, it can still be habit-forming. The Dutch policy toward marijuana suggests it is possible to take away some of marijuana's allure, particularly among young people. Indeed, proponents of marijuana legalization trust that it will.

David Musto, a historian on drug policy, suggests that public attitudes go through regular cycles. First, a small group of people experiment with a new drug. They promote it. The drug's popularity grows. Then the public learns about its dangers. As a result, the drug is prohibited, while the populace grows intolerant of those who abuse it. Then the drug's negative image spreads to the poor. Finally, use declines.

According to Musto, the present crack epidemic closely resembles a previous cocaine epidemic that lasted from 1885 to the 1920s. If there is a lesson to learn from history, it is that, like its predecessor, the current crack epidemic will eventually wind down. However, Musto predicts that it will take at least another decade.

Other experts agree that drug use is cyclical, but they argue that it will decrease regardless of the laws. Arnold Trebach, founder of the Drug Policy Foundation, pointed out that with the exception of fourteen years of Prohibition, alcohol has always been part of the American heritage—and legal. In 1830, Americans consumed more liquor than ever before or after, reaching a high point of more than seven gallons absolute proof per person.[8] By the end of the 1800s, consumption dropped to less than two gallons per person. "These changes," noted Trebach, "took place within an atmosphere of legality."

Theories like Trebach's ignore the influx of immigrants and what contribution they may have had on the social landscape. They also ignore the rise in drinking when Prohibition was repealed, as well as the widespread alcoholism, compulsive gambling, and cigarette addiction that exist now, despite the legality of the products and activities.

WOULD ADDICTION INCREASE OR DECREASE?

During the past decade, Americans became more health conscious. Their increased awareness contributed to a decline in smoking and drinking. Smoking declined from 40 percent of all Americans in 1965 to only 29 percent in 1988. Drinking also declined; distilled spirit consumption is down 25 percent.[9]

Millions of Americans are getting the message about illicit drugs as well. In 1988, the National Household Survey found that current drug use (at least once a month) had dropped by a third in just a few years. For all combined drug use between 1985 and 1988, nine million fewer Americans used drugs. Among cocaine users, the drop was even greater. In 1988, only half as many people used cocaine as in 1985.[10]

Unfortunately, the numbers for crack were dismal. For the same period, frequent crack use (daily or weekly) had nearly doubled, to almost one million Americans. In addition, there were many innocent victims of drug use. In 1988, 200,000 babies were born to mothers on drugs; half of those were to mothers on crack.[11]

It could be argued, though not everyone would agree, that

125

all illicit drug use is harmful. But despite the serious problems habitual users have or inflict on others, not all users are drug addicts. Why they aren't remains in large part a mystery. That some are, however, is one of the most compelling reasons for drug control. That is one of the most worrisome risks to legalization—that there would be more drug use and therefore more drug abuse and addiction. How far will addiction rates spiral upward if drugs were legalized?

An obvious predictor is to look at drugs that are already legal. Based on their addiction rates, we can make predictions about drug legalization and its potential effect on the number of addicts.

Currently more than 60 million Americans smoke cigarettes and 100 million Americans drink liquor.[12] As with illicit drugs, not all smokers and drinkers are addicted to nicotine and alcohol; a portion can quit at will. However, among smokers, addiction is extremely high; practically all regular smokers are addicted to nicotine. Even though smoking has declined in recent years, half of those who currently smoke report having tried to quit and failed.[13] The other half didn't even try.

Alcohol is far less addictive than nicotine. Still, one in ten regular drinkers becomes dependent on alcohol. Given the huge number of drinkers in America, that translates to 10.5 million alcoholics.

Research has found that most controlled drugs are less addictive than nicotine but more addictive than alcohol. Cocaine, for example, is one of the most worrisome drugs because it is so addictive. One reason for its addictiveness is that when it is taken, it almost instantly gives users pleasure, a pleasure many of them seek again and again.

In one laboratory experiment, rats were given unlimited access to cocaine. The rats preferred taking cocaine to eating or sleeping. They also took increasingly larger amounts until they died from overdosing.[14] While it is impossible to draw exact parallels to humans, we know that cocaine addiction is high, crack addiction even higher.

Studies show that it takes a few years for signs of cocaine

addiction to become apparent. According to Dr. Jack Henningfield of the Baltimore Addiction Research Center, the odds of crack addiction are one in six. Other experts place it twice as high, at one in three.

In 1988, the National Institute of Drug Abuse estimated that 14.5 million Americans used drugs regularly, at least once a month. Of those, 4 million had what NIDA defined as a "serious drug problem" (they used drugs at least 200 times that year). Between 1.7 million and 2 million were actually addicted to drugs.

Based on the rate of addiction, if drugs, especially cocaine and heroin, were legalized, the number of addicts could increase at least tenfold to 20 million. Some experts place the "at risk" population at 12 percent of the total U.S. population, or about 29 million people.[15] A few experts suggest that the potential number of addicts may even be as high as 50 million to 60 million.

COULD TREATMENT MEET THE INCREASED DEMAND?

Jeff had just been released from prison after serving a sentence for drug dealing to support his habit. After prison, he could only afford to live in public housing. As in most large cities, drug use was rampant. So Jeff wanted to get into a residential drug-rehabilitation program as soon as possible.

Private treatment was available, but Jeff could not afford it. He turned instead to a publicly funded program. Administrators informed him that the waiting period for admission to the program was six months. Thus, Jeff faced six more months in the housing project, amid drugs, temptation, and despair.

Jeff's story is no exception. Knowing of the long wait, many addicts do not even bother applying for treatment. Dr. Robert G. Newman, who operates the largest methadone maintenance treatment program in the country, says that 20,000 to 50,000 addicts would seek treatment immediately if they were convinced it was available.[16]

Currently, the nation provides only 250,000 treatment slots

in about 5,000 programs.[17] Nationally, only about 80 percent of the slots are ever filled. However, the vacancies are in the private slots; there is an acute shortage of publicly funded ones. In some parts of the country, the shortage is severe.

In New York, for example, it is estimated that there are almost 900,000 addicts (this does not include marijuana users). But the state offers only 50,000 treatment slots.[18]

Irving Shandler has worked for the homeless for over twenty-six years. His experience has taught him that drug abuse is one of the major causes of homelessness. In 1989, Los Angeles had 50,000 to 1,000,000 homeless people. If Shandler is correct, and by most reports he is, then thousands were in need of treatment. Yet the city provided only twenty-five beds in residential treatment centers for the homeless.[19]

Like Jeff, most addicts cannot afford treatment, and thus far, the public has failed to foot many of their bills. Depending on the number that require long-term care, the cost for treating the current number of addicts is already between $8 billion and $30 billion.[20]

As we discussed earlier, tax revenues from legalized drugs could amount to $10 billion, but that is nowhere near what it would take to treat 20, 30, or even 60 million new addicts. Who is going to make up the difference?

Residential treatment programs cost only half as much as imprisoning drug abusers. Ironically, despite an increase, the most recent federal budget allocates far more funds for prison cells than treatment slots.

Even if all serious drug users underwent treatment and rehabilitation, it would still leave us with a large population of addicts. Why? Chemical dependency has no permanent cure; the battle against it is lifelong. Relapse is always a real possibility.

Furthermore, despite medical advances and new treatments from methadone to acupuncture, there is no treatment known to be 100 percent successful. Even if there were, not all drug abusers are ready or willing to undergo it. In fact, evidence suggests that a substantial number don't.

If drugs were legalized, what is there to suggest that the

128

shortage of treatment programs will disappear, that there will be sufficient funds to pay for treatment, that treatment will be effective, and that everyone who needs it will agree to it?

This look at drugs began by watching Sisyphus roll his rock up the mountain again and again. Perhaps it might conclude with a look at Pandora.

Pandora was given a sealed box from the gods and goddesses who warned her not to open it. But one day, out of curiosity, she did. Out of the box flew a buzzing cloud of evil that flew into the world to plague humanity.

Unlike Sisyphus's rock, Pandora's problem was not hers alone, for the evil flying out of her box belonged to the world. And belonging to the world, it belonged to each person in it.

Such is the saga of drugs. The problem is not just that of inner cities and distant drug-producing nations. It belongs to each of us, to everyone. For its effects ripple into many aspects of our lives, from our nation's economy to our own safety from crime.

Pandora's box was never empty, though. What was still inside was hope. No matter how evil a problem, hope gives the ability to endure. We may not yet have discovered a solution to the drug problem. In fact, we may never find one. But not one among us needs give up hope.

Laws can never tell a complete story, and drug laws are no exception. Like alcohol prohibition, they have failed to stop use. Like it, too, they have probably kept abuse down.

Still, crime is up. Drug crimes cost dearly, both in money and human misery.

Each side of the drug-legalization debate makes valid arguments. And harbors rational fears.

The dilemma is not which side prevails. Rather, it is which course we set for society. Which problems we choose to tolerate. And which problems we think we can manage.

For most Americans, legalizing drugs is a dangerous gamble they are unwilling to risk. But a few, many of them experts on the issue, believe it a risk worth taking.

APPENDIX

1803	morphine discovered
1839–42	the Opium Wars fought between China and England
1898	heroin (diacetylmorphin) first distributed by Bayer Company, a German firm
1906	Pure Food and Drug Act requiring truthful labeling
1909	Shanghai conference; on February 9, 1909, an anti-opium smoking bill was signed into law. Prohibited the importation and use of opium for other than medicinal purposes.
1912	Hague Convention—first international treaty restricting drugs was signed
1914	December 14, 1914, Harrison Narcotic Act
1924	Harrison Act was revised to prohibit heroin
1937	Marijuana Tax Act banning cannabis
1962	White House Conference on Narcotics and Drug Abuse to examine the problem
1968	creation of Federal Bureau of Narcotics and Dangerous Drugs (BNDD) in the Justice Department to enforce drug laws
1970	first "War on Drugs" declared by President Richard M. Nixon
	passage of Controlled Substance Act (CSA), which provided a uniform drug law; the Single Convention, an international treaty, eventually signed by 138 nations
1973	creation of Drug Enforcement Agency (DEA) through

	merger of several federal agencies; Nixon declared a victory in the War on Drugs
1973–79	eleven states decriminalized possession of small amounts of marijuana
1982	creation of Presidential Task Force in Southern Florida to combat drug imports from Latin America and the Caribbean
1984	Second War on Drugs declared by President Ronald Reagan; Omnibus Drug Bill
1989	Creation of Drug Czar post by President Bush. Heightened concern of crack epidemic, which led to escalation of War on Drugs

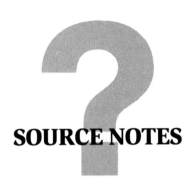

SOURCE NOTES

CHAPTER ONE

1. A federal study showed that in 1985 overall drug use declined by 37 percent. On the other hand, crack and anabolic steroid use increased. "Bennett's Drug War," *Newsweek*, 21 August 1989, 16; and Hagan, "Athletes Seek Winning Edge by Using Drug," *Cleveland Plain Dealer*, 16 July 1989.
2. Buckley, "Legalize Dope," *Washington Post*, 1 April 1985.
3. Nizer, "How About Low-Cost Drugs for Addicts?" Undated Op-Ed piece from ACLU files.
4. Rangel, "Legalize Drugs? Not on Your Life," *New York Times*, 17 May 1988.
5. "Bennett's Drug War," *Newsweek*, 21 August 1989, 17.
6. Hershey, "Drug War," *New York Times*, 18 August 1989.
7. Select Committee on Narcotics Abuse and Control, U.S. House of Representatives Monthly Narcotics Report, September 1988.
8. Winer, "Poll Finds Public Favors Tougher Laws Against Drug Sale and Use," *New York Times*, 15 August 1989.
9. Gravely, "Building the Case Against America's Jihad," *In These Times*, 14 December 1988, 10.
10. Riding, "Western Panel Is Asking End to All Curbs on Drug Traffic," *New York Times*, 2 February 1989.

CHAPTER TWO

1. Courtwright, *Dark Paradise*, 43.
2. Ibid., 51.

3. Courtwright, 58.
4. Brecher, *Licit, Illicit Drugs,* 3.
5. Grauer, *Drugs and the Law,* 55; and Brecher, 270.
6. Cited in Courtwright, 97.
7. Musto, *American Disease,* 282 (footnote 13). It is estimated that 0.2 percent of the population was addicted to drugs, although some of the politicians set it inaccurately high at upwards of 3 percent or one million people.
8. Brecher, 49.
9. *Webb, et al.* v. *United States,* cited in Musto, 132.

CHAPTER THREE

1. Kleiman, "Vice Policy in a Liberal Society," *Nova Law Review,* 949; and Egan, "Pain Recruited in War on Drunk Driving," *New York Times,* 16 March 1989.
2. Berke, "After Studying for War on Drugs, Bennett Wants More Troops," *New York Times,* 6 August 1989.
3. Kidwell, "The War on Drugs," *The New American,* 7 November 1988, 31.
4. "Casual Drug Use Is Sharply Down," *New York Times,* 1 August 1989.
5. The White House, *National Drug Control Strategy Report,* September 1989, 75.1.
6. Ibid.
7. Quoted in Boyd, "Bush Seeks Mandatory Execution in Slaying of Federal Law Officers," *New York Times,* 10 March 1989.
8. Quoted in Musto, *American Disease,* 267.

CHAPTER FOUR

1. *Reason,* October 1988, 22–29.
2. Frank Apisa, Letter to the Editor, *New York Times,* 6 February 1989.
3. The testimony of experts before the House Select Committee on Narcotics in September 1988 has been summarized in the September 1988 issue of *Drug Abuse Update,* the monthly newsletter published by the National Drug Information Center of Families in Action and the Scott Newman Center.
4. Trebach, "Practical Advice on Drug Legalization," unpublished paper delivered to the House hearings on legalization in September 1988, 3.
5. Muro, "If Drugs Were Legal," *Boston Globe,* 12 June 1988.

6. Englesman, "The Dutch Model," Drug Policy Foundation Conference, October 1989, taped lecture.

CHAPTER FIVE

1. The National Organization for the Reform of Marijuana Laws (NORML) pamphlet, 1987.
2. Kidwell, "The War on Drugs, *American Opinion,* 7 November 1988, 33.
3. John Stuart Mill, *On Liberty,* 1859, lines 335–351.
4. Wisotsky, House Hearings on Legalization, 29 September 1988, prepared statement, 10.
5. Wisotsky, *Nova Law Review,* 897.
6. Wade, "Knowing the Rules of the Road Wherever You Are," *New York Times,* 19 March 1989.
7. U.S. Dept. of Health and Human Services, National Household Survey on Drug Abuse: Population Estimates 1988, Washington, D.C., 1989. Table 2–A, 17.
8. Kaplan, *The Hardest Drug,* 107.
9. 130 Congressional Record, 118, H9765 (daily edition, 19 September 1984). Cited in Stoll, "Why Not Heroin?" *Journal of Contemporary Health, Law and Policy,* Spring 1985.
10. Cited in Stoll, *Washington Times,* 28 March 1984.
11. "Rights, Repressions and Reform," Drug Policy Foundation Conference, 1988, tape.
12. Wisotsky, "The Drug Crackdown: Trashing the Bill of Rights," unpublished paper, 25.
13. Ibid.
14. Myers, "Akron to Check on Drugs," *Akron Beacon Journal,* 25 February 1989.
15. Cramer, "Eyes in the Sky," *Time,* 6 February 1989.
16. Hirn, "Drug Tests Threaten Employers, Too," *New York Times,* 12 November 1988.
17. Rosecan, "Hair Testing Not Valid for Cocaine Abuse" (Letter to the Editor), *New York Times,* 31 October 1988.
18. Dougherty, "Controversies Regarding Urine Testing," *Journal of Substance Abuse Treatment* 4 (1987): 116.
19. Ibid.
20. Dougherty, op. cit.

CHAPTER SIX

1. Kidwell, "The War on Drugs," *New Americans,* 7 November 1988, 31.

134

2. "Getting Gangsters Out of Drugs," *The Economist*, 2 April 1988, 11.
3. Mohr, "Deaths and Arrests Mount, but the Drug Trade Is Flourishing," *New York Times*, 1 February 1989.
4. Berke, "Drug Rings Turn Border Into a Vast Route to U.S.," *New York Times*, 27 August 1989.
5. Nadelman, "U.S. Policy: A Bad Export," *Foreign Policy*, Spring 1988, 89.
6. Morganthau and Miller, "Now It's Bush's War," *Newsweek*, 18 September 1989, 24.
7. "Addiction in America," *Lears*, January/February 1989, 59; and Kolbert, "Treating Drug Addicts: Who Should Pay for It?" *New York Times*, 2 February 1989.
8. Belkin, "Drug Tax Aiming at Snaring Dealers," *New York Times*, 26 August 1989.
9. Kolbert, "Treating Addicts."
10. Blakeslee, "Crack's Toll Among Babies: Joyless View, Even of Toys," *New York Times*, 17 September 1989.
11. Bishop, "Gap Between Cost of Drug Epidemic and State Money Shuts California Clinic," *New York Times*, 3 February 1989; and Morganthau, "Drug Habits We Can't Afford," *New York Times*, 14 December 1988.
12. Nadelman, op. cit., 88.
13. Brooke, "Attacking the Sovereign State of Cocaine," *New York Times*, 27 August 1989.
14. Clarke, "Legalizing Drugs—Step No. 1," *New York Times*, 26 August 1989.
15. Christian, "Bolivia Shifts Tactics in Drug Fight," *New York Times*, 19 March 1989.
16. Brooke, "Peruvian Farmers Razing Rain Forest to Sow Drug Crops," *New York Times*, 13 August 1989.
17. Christian, "Bolivia Shifts Tactics in Drug Fight," *New York Times*, 19 March 1989.
18. Courtwright, *Dark Paradise*, 83.
19. Koch testimony before House Select Committee on Narcotics Abuse and Control, September 29, 1988.

CHAPTER SEVEN

1. "Casual Drug Use Is Sharply Down," *New York Times*, 1 August 1989.
2. Kahler, "Despite Billions Spent in Fight, America Not Saying No to Drugs," *New York Times*, 27 August 1989.

3. U.S. Department of Justice Research in Action Newsletter, reprinted from *NIJ Report,* March/April 1988, 2.
4. Marriott, "After 3 Years, Crack Plague in New York Grows Worse," *New York Times,* 20 February 1989.
5. Ayres, "At Last, Crime Too Heavy for Capital to Bear," *New York Times,* 22 March 1989.
6. Attorney General Richard Thornburgh, quoted in "Federal Drug Sweep Hits Jamaican Gang," *Cleveland Plain Dealer,* 11 October 1988.
7. Terry, "Drug Riches of the Capital Luring Poor Youths Down a Bloody Path," *New York Times,* 31 March 1989.
8. Griffith, " 'Roid Rages' Can Turn Users into Abusers, Killers," *Cleveland Plain Dealer,* 17 July 1989.
9. Griffith, op. cit.
10. Roberts, "Substance Abuse Among Men Who Batter Their Mates," *Journal of Substance Abuse Treatment* 5 (1988): 83.
11. "Addiction in America," *Lears,* January/February 1989, 59.
12. Buckley, "Inmate's Viewpoint on Legalized Drugs Carries Ring of Truth," United Press wire story, September 1985.
13. Ostrowski, "Why Cocaine and Heroin Should be Decriminalized," Advisory Report of the Committee on Law Reform of the New York County Lawyers Association, 29 April 1987, 30.
14. Boaz, "The Legalization of Drugs," *Vital Speeches of the Day,* 15 August 1988, 656.
15. Clarke, "Legalizing Drugs—Step No. 1," *New York Times,* 26 August 1989.
16. Terry, "Bystander, 12, Is Shot and Killed in Drug Dispute," *New York Times,* 22 January 1989; and Hevesi, "In Drug Wars, Innocent Die," *New York Times,* 22 January 1989.
17. "A DEA Hero Is Busted," *Newsweek,* 28 August 1989, 32.
18. Boaz, op. cit.

CHAPTER EIGHT

1. Berke, "A Record 14 Officers Killed in '88 in Drug Incidents, a Study Shows," *New York Times,* 3 September 1989.
2. Smith, "The Soldier's Story," *Reason,* August/September 1988, 32.
3. Reuter, "Can the Borders Be Sealed?" *Public Interest,* Summer 1988, 52.
4. Berke, "Drug Rings Turn Border Into a Vast Route to U.S.," *New York Times,* 27 August 1989.

5. The White House, *National Drug Control Strategy Report,* September 1989, 73.
6. Berke, op. cit.
7. Berke, "Attack on Airborne Drug Smuggling Called Ineffective," *New York Times,* 9 June 1989.
8. Berke, "New Form of Interstate Commerce: Drugs Are Stealing Through U.S.," *New York Times,* 28 August 1989.
9. Reuter, op. cit.
10. *Prisoners in 1988,* U.S. Department of Justice Statistics Bulletin, 1.
11. Pitt, "Drug Cases Clog New York Courts," *New York Times,* 4 April 1989.
12. Marriott, "After 3 Years, Crack Plague in New York Grows Worse," *New York Times,* 20 February 1989.
13. "What the Plan Would Aim to Do." *New York Times,* 3 September 1989.

CHAPTER NINE

1. Morganthau, "Hitting the Drug Lords," *Newsweek,* 4 September 1989, 34. These statistics actually include both the Medellín group and its rival, the Cali cartel.
2. Treaster, "Colombian Policemen and Soldiers Are Reportedly Tipping off Drug Figures," *New York Times,* 4 September 1989.
3. Kidwell, "The War on Drugs," *New Americans,* 34.
4. Hsein Chou Liu, *The Development of a Single Convention on Narcotic Drugs* (Bangkok: Academy of New Society, 1979): 3, 16.
5. *United States International Drug Control Activities Report,* 1988, 11.
6. *Drugs, Law Enforcement and Foreign Policy,* a report prepared by the Subcommittee on Terrorism, Narcotics and International Operations for the Senate Foreign Relations Committee, December 1988, p. 32.
7. Szulc, "Join with Castro to Fight Drugs," *New York Times,* 9 August 1989.
8. Linda Greenhouse, "Court to Decide on Foreign Searches," *New York Times,* 18 April 1989.
9. Brooke, "Peruvian Farmers Razing Rain Forest to Sow Drug Crops," *New York Times,* 13 August 1989.
10. Passell, "How the Traffickers Profited from the War on Marijuana," *New York Times,* 5 September 1989.

137

CHAPTER TEN

1. Kidwell, "The War on Drugs," *New Americans,* 7 November 1988, 32.
2. Zimmerman, Letter to the Editor, *New York Times,* 31 March 1988. (Mr. Zimmerman was attorney general of Pennsylvania.)
3. The White House, *National Drug Control Strategy Report,* September 1989, 7.
4. Kaplan, "Taking Drugs Seriously, *Public Interest,* Summer 1988, 41.
5. National Institute on Drug Abuse, *Illicit Drug Use, Smoking, and Drinking by America's High School Students, College Students and Young Adults 1975–1987.*
6. Heard, "Arguments against Legalizing Drugs," *Drug Abuse Update,* September 1988, 28.
7. White House, op. cit., 11.
8. Cited in both Arnold Trebach's and Charles Rangel's statements in Congressional hearings in September 1988.
9. According to *Impact,* the liquor industry's journal, beer consumption is down 7 percent, wine is down 14 percent, and distilled spirits consumption is down 23 percent. Hall, "A New Temperance Is Taking Root in America," *New York Times,* 15 March 1989.
10. 1985 National Household Survey on Drug Abuse: Population Estimates, 54. 1988 National Household Survey on Drug Abuse: Population Estimates, 17.
11. White House, op. cit., 2.
12. According to the 1988 National Household Survey on Drug Abuse, 149 million Americans had tried cigarettes in their lifetime; 57 million had smoked it in the month prior to the survey; 168 million had tried alcohol in their lifetime, and 106 million had taken a drink in the month of the survey. 1988 National Household Survey on Drug Abuse, 89, 83.
13. Carter, "Keep Costs of Illegal Drug Use in Perspective," *Wall Street Journal,* 14 August 1986. About 55 million Americans smoke; 85 percent say they would like to quit; 61 percent have tried to quit and failed.
14. Julio Martinez, director of New York State Services of Substance Abuse, Congressional Hearings, September 1988. In 1965, 49 percent of the population smoked; by 1988 the number had declined to 29 percent. But among teenage girls and other select groups, consumption actually increased.

15. Morganthau and Miller, "Hour by Hour Crack," *Newsweek*, 28 November 1988, 77.
16. Mariott, "Treatment for Addicts Is as Elusive as Ever," *New York Times*, 9 July 1989.
17. White House, op. cit., 36, 39.
18. Mariott, op. cit.
19. Kolata, "Twins of the Streets: Homelessness and Addiction," *New York Times*, 22 May 1989.
20. Morganthau and Miller, op. cit., 71.

GLOSSARY

addict: a person dependent on drugs

convention: treaty or agreement

contraband: illegal goods

decriminalization: when violation of a law is treated as a civil instead of a criminal offense

de facto legalization: when law enforcement ignores a law

drug abuser: a person dependent on drugs

drug cartel: an organization of drug traffickers

drug control policy: the various ways a government goes about controlling the drug problem

drug czar: director of the federal drug policy agency

drug runner: a person engaged in transporting drugs

drug user: a person using drugs

eradication: destruction of illegally grown drug crops, for example, by spraying herbicides

extradition: surrendering a suspect to another jurisdiction or country for prosecution

iatrogenic addiction: doctor-caused addiction

interdiction: seizing drugs in transit or upon arrival at a country's border

legalization: repeal of laws against recreational drug use

money laundering: funneling the cash profits from illegal drug sales into legitimate bank accounts, businesses, and other operations

mule: a person smuggling drugs across borders

posse: term used to describe members of drug gangs

141

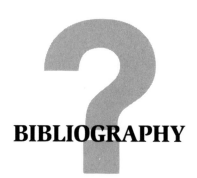

BIBLIOGRAPHY

A DEA hero is busted. 1989. *Newsweek* (28 August):32.

Addiction in America, 1989. *Lears* (January/February):59.

America after Prohibition: The next debate over drug legalization. 1988. *Reason* (October):22–29.

Anti-drug smuggling mission ends with helicopter crash. 1988. *Cleveland Plain Dealer* (26 October).

Apisa, Frank. 1989. A new medicine. Letter to Editor. *New York Times* (4 March).

Arguments against legalizing drugs. 1988. *Drug Abuse Update.* National Drug Information Center of Families in Action and the Scott Newman Center (September).

Ayres, B. Drummond, Jr. 1989. At last, crime too heavy for Capital to bear. *New York Times* (22 March).

Azzam, Abraham L. 1981. SAO/SWA: Mounting the U.S. response. *Drug Enforcement* (Summer):22–24.

Bacon, John. 1981. Is the French Connection really dead? *Drug Enforcement* (Summer):19–21.

Bain, David Haward. 1989. Book review of *Kings of Cocaine* by Guy Gugliotta and Jeff Leen. *New York Times Book Review* (30 April):13.

Belkin, Lisa. 1989. Drug tax aiming at snaring dealers. *New York Times* (26 August).

Bellows, Kevin. 1989. Legalizing drugs: Proposals and prospects. *Lears* (March):104.

Berke, Richard L. 1989. After studying for War on Drugs, Bennett wants more troops. *New York Times* (6 August).

142

—. 1989. Bennett asks tougher drug fight, declaring crack 'biggest problem.' *New York Times* (1 August).

—. 1989. Drug rings turn border into a vast route to U.S. *New York Times* (27 August).

—. 1989. Foreign policy said to hinder drug war. *New York Times* (14 April).

—. 1989. New form of interstate commerce: Drugs are stealing through U.S. *New York Times* (28 August).

—. 1989. Official corruption grows as drug smuggling flourishes *New York Times* (29 August).

—. 1989. The post-arrest drug test gets a foothold. *New York Times* (2 April).

—. 1989. U.S. plans 4-mile ditch on border to stem drug flow to California. *New York Times* (26 January).

Biermans, John T. 1988. *Why cocaine and heroin should not be decriminalized.* Unpublished advisory report of the Committee on Law Reform, New York County Lawyers Association.

Bishop, Katherine. 1989. Gap between cost of drug epidemic and state money shuts California clinic. *New York Times* (3 February).

Blakeslee, Sandra. 1989. Crack's toll among babies: Joyless view, even of toys. *New York Times* (17 September).

Boaz, David, 1988. The legalization of drugs: Decriminalization. *Vital Speeches* (15 August).

Booth, Cathy. 1988. Tentacles of the octopus: The Mafia brings Europe's worst drug epidemic home. *Time* (12 December):48.

Boyd, Gerald M. 1989. Bush seeks mandatory execution in slaying of federal law officer. *New York Times* (10 March).

Brecher, Edward M., ed. 1972. *Licit and Illicit Drugs.* Boston: Little, Brown.

Brooke, James. 1989. Bogota's hottest tour: Pleasure domes of the cartels. *New York Times* (30 August).

—. 1989. Colombian drug cartels tied to terror in rights report. *New York Times* (6 April).

—. 1989. Death threats terrorize the courts in Colombia. *New York Times* (27 August).

—. 1989. Peruvian farmers razing rain forest to sow drug crops. *New York Times* (13 August).

Buckley, William F., Jr. 1986. Legalize dope. *Washington Post* (1 April).

Casual drug use is sharply down. 1989. *New York Times* (1 August).

Chavkin, Wendy. 1989. Help, don't jail addicted mothers. *Cleveland Plain Dealer* (18 July).

143

Christian, Shirley. 1989. Bolivia shifts tactics in drug fight. *New York Times* (19 March).

Church, George. 1988. Should drugs be made legal? *Time* (30 May):12–19.

Clarke, Kildare. 1989. Legalizing drugs/Step No. 1. *New York Times* (26 August).

Cohen, Sidney. 1985. Is legalization the answer? *Drug Abuse and Alcoholism* (August).

Colombia arrests 4,000 after slaying. 1989. *New York Times* (21 August).

Colombians seize drug ring suspect and 134 aircraft. 1989. *New York Times* (22 August).

Court continues privacy erosion. 1989. *The Drug Policy Letter* (March/April):3–4.

Courtwright, David T. 1982. *Dark paradise: Opiate addiction in America before 1940*. Cambridge, Mass.: Harvard University Press.

Cowan, Richard C. 1988. Beyond the War on Drugs. *Orange County Register* (12 June).

Cramer, Jerome. 1989. Eyes in the sky. *Time* (6 February):60.

Cushman, John H., Jr. 1989. A call for testing all transit workers. *New York Times* (7 May).

Demand-side drug fix. 1988. *U.S. News and World Report* (14 March).

DiCarlo, Dominick L. 1982. International initiatives to control coca production and cocaine trafficking. *Drug Enforcement* (Fall):6–9.

Dolan, Edward F., Jr. 1985. *International Drug Traffic*. New York: Franklin Watts.

Dougherty, Ronald J. 1987. Controversies regarding urine-testing. *Journal of Substance Abuse Treatment* 4:115–17.

———. 1984. Status of cocaine abuse. *Journal of Substance Abuse Treatment* 1:157–161.

Drug arrests and the courts' pleas for help. 1989. *New York Times* (9 April).

Drug Policy Foundation International Conference. 1988 (October). Tapes of all sessions.

Drugs, Law Enforcement and Foreign Policy. 1988. A report prepared by the Subcommittee on Terrorism, Narcotics and International Operations for the Senate Foreign Relations Committee (Dec.).

Drunkenness, gambling, pot smoking . . . behind the trend to go easy on "victimless crimes." 1976. *U.S. News and World Report* (15 November):80.

Eastern's plane returned following cocaine seizure. 1988. *Cleveland Plain Dealer* (26 October).

144

Egan, Timothy. 1989. Pain recruited in War on Drunk Driving. *New York Times* (16 March).

Eldridge, William Butler. 1967. *Narcotics and the Law,* 2nd ed. Chicago: University of Chicago Press.

Farkas, Karen. 1989. Browns' Mack pleads guilty. *Cleveland Plain Dealer* (31 August).

Federal drug sweep hits Jamaican gangs. 1988. *Cleveland Plain Dealer* (11 October).

Foderaro, Lisa W. 1989. Hundreds mourn slain drug fighter in Brooklyn. *New York Times* (13 August).

Former dictator favored as Bolivians vote today. 1989. *Cleveland Plain Dealer* (7 May).

Gallup, George, Jr., and Alex Gallup. 1988. Americans show widespread opposition to drug legalization. Press release. Princeton, N.J.: Gallup Poll (31 July).

Geis, Gilbert. 1972. *Not the law's business? An examination of homosexuality, abortion, prostitution, narcotics and gambling in the U.S.* Rockville, Md.: National Institute of Mental Health.

Getting gangsters out of drugs. 1988. *The Economist* (2 April):11–12.

Gladwell, Malcolm. 1986. A new addiction to an old story. *Insight: The Washington Times Magazine* (27 October):8–12.

Grace, Beth. 1989. Losing ground against crack. *Akron Beacon Journal* (30 January).

Grauer, Neil A. 1988. *Drugs and the Law.* New York: Chelsea House.

Gravley, Eric. 1988. Building the case against America's narcotic jihad. *In These Times* (14 December).

Greenhouse, Linda. 1989. Court backs tests of some workers to deter drug use. *New York Times* (21 March).

———. 1989. Court to decide foreign searches. *New York Times* (18 April).

———. 1989. Justices to hear case on drugs in religions. *New York Times* (21 March).

Griffith, John. 1989. 'Roid rages' can turn users into abusers, killers. *Cleveland Plain Dealer* (17 July).

Guenther, Wally. 1989. Cocaine problem growing in area. *Cleveland Plain Dealer* (30 April).

Hagan, John F., and John Griffith. 1989. Steroids. *Cleveland Plain Dealer* (16–17 July).

Hall, Trish. 1989. A new temperance is taking root in America. *New York Times* (15 March).

Hamill, Peter. 1988. Facing up to drugs: Is legalization the solution? *New York Magazine* (15 August):20–27.

145

Henderson, Karen H. 1988. Cracking down on cocaine. *Cleveland Plain Dealer* (23 October).

Hershy, Robert D., Jr. 1989. Drug war. *New York Times* (18 August).

Hevesi, Dennis. 1989. In drug wars, innocent die. *New York Times* (12 January).

Hidley, William C. 1989. Acupuncture for addicts. *Cleveland Plain Dealer* (28 March).

Hirn, Richard J. 1988. Drug tests threaten employers, too. *New York Times* (12 November).

Hogan, Phoebe. 1989. Getting clean: A new generation fights addiction. *New York Times* (20 February):38–45.

Hobbs, Michael. 1988. Rock City, where crack is the king. *Cleveland Plain Dealer* (30 October).

House Select Committee on Narcotics Abuse and Control Hearings Transcripts. 1988 (29 September). Transcripts include: Rep. Charles B. Rangel, Rep. Benjamin Gilman, Edward Koch, Julio A. Martinez, Charles R. Schuster, Arnold S. Trebach, Jerald R. Vaughn, Admiral James D. Watkins, Steven Wisotsky, Gloria Whitfield, and Raymond Whitfield.

Kahler, Kathryn. 1989. 'Crack' gains as cocaine substitute. *Cleveland Plain Dealer* (31 August).

―――. 1989. Despite billions spent in fight, America not saying no to drugs. *Cleveland Plain Dealer* (27 August).

―――. 1989. More drug treatment centers urged. *Cleveland Plain Dealer* (29 August).

―――. 1989. U.S. jails, courts under heavy fire from war on drugs. *Cleveland Plain Dealer* (28 August).

Kaplan, John. 1983. *The Hardest Drug: Heroin and Public Policy.* Chicago: University of Chicago Press.

―――. 1988. Taking drugs seriously. *Public Interest* (Summer).

Kerr, Peter. 1988. The unspeakable is debated: Should drugs be legalized? *New York Times Magazine* (15 May).

Kidwell, Kirk. 1988. The war on drugs. *New Americans* (7 November).

Kifner, John. 1989. In war on crack, undercover soldiers battle street by street. *New York Times* (22 February).

Koch, Edward I. 1989. For anti-drug boot camps. *New York Times* (24 May).

Kolata, Gina. 1989. Experts finding new hope on treating crack addicts. *New York Times* (24 August).

―――. 1989. Medications may ease craving for cocaine. *New York Times* (7 March).

————. 1989. Twins of the streets: Homelessness and addiction. *New York Times* (22 May).

Kolbert, Elizabeth. 1989. Treating drug addicts: Who should pay for it? *New York Times* (24 February).

Kooyman, Martien, M.D. 1984. Drug problem in the Netherlands. *Journal of Substance Abuse Treatment* (1):125–130.

Levine, Richard. 1989. Undercover officer buying drugs is shot in Bronx. *New York Times* (11 August).

Liu, Hsein Chou. 1979. *The development of a Single Convention on Narcotic Drugs.* Bangkok, Thailand: Academy of New Society.

Lyall, Sarah, 1989. Bronx mother slain over crack money, police say. *New York Times* (7 January).

Lyle, John P. 1981. Southwest Asian heroin. *Drug Enforcement* (Summer).

Marriott, Michael. 1989. After 3 years, crack plague in New York grows worse. *New York Times* (20 February).

————. 1989. Treatment for addicts is as elusive as ever. *New York Times* (9 July).

Marshall, Elliot. 1988. Drug wars: Legalization gets a hearing. *News & Comment* (2 September).

————. 1988. *Legalization: A Debate.* New York: Chelsea House.

McFadden, Robert D. 1989. Federal Drug Agency takes center stage. *New York Times* (10 March).

McKinley, James C., Jr. 1989. Constant reality in Bronx housing project: Fear of violent drug gangs. *New York Times* (15 May).

————. 1989. Informer warned police of robbery. *New York Times* (17 August).

Model Drug Paraphernalia Act: Can we outlaw head shops and should we? 1981. *Georgia Law Review* (Fall):137–169.

Mohr, Charles. 1989. Deaths and arrests mount, but the drug trade is flourishing. *New York Times* (1 February).

————. 1988. Penalty of death kept in drug bill. *New York Times* (14 October).

Molotsky, Irvin. 1988. Capital's homicide rate is at a record. *New York Times* (30 October).

Mondzac, Allen M., M.D. 1984. In defense of the reintroduction of heroin into American medical practice and H.R. 5290: The Compassionate Pain Relief Act. *New England Journal of Medicine* (23 August).

Morganthau, Robert M. 1989. Drug habits we can't afford. *New York Times* (14 December).

Morganthau, Tom. 1989. Now the fight is with blood: Colombia decides to allow the U.S. to extradite. *Newsweek* (28 August):37.

———— and Mark Miller. 1988. Hour by hour: Crack. *Newsweek* (28 November):64–79.

Muro, Mark. 1988. If drugs were legal. *Boston Globe* (12 June).

Musto, David F., M.D. 1987. *The American Disease: Origins of Narcotic Control.* New York: Oxford University Press.

Myers, Marcia. 1989. Akron to check on drugs. *Akron Beacon Journal* (25 February).

Nadelman, Ethan A. 1988. The case for legalization. *Public Interest* (Summer):3–31.

————. 1988. U.S. drug policy: A bad export. *Foreign Policy* (Spring):83–108.

National Committee on Treatment of Intractable Pain Newsletter. 1988. (Winter).

National Institute on Drug Abuse. 1988. *Illicit drug use, smoking, and drinking among America's high school students, college students, and young adults. 1975–1987.* Washington, D.C.: U.S. Department of Health and Human Services.

————. 1988. *National Household Survey on Drug Abuse: Main Findings 1985.* Washington, D.C.: U.S. Department of Health and Human Services.

A national town meeting: The legalization of drugs. 1988. *The Koppel Report.* Transcript (13 September).

New addition to an old story. 1986. *Insight: The Washington Times* (27 October).

New drug law: The Senate's duty. Editorial. 1988. *New York Times* (4 October).

New York's drug lesson for America. Editorial. 1989. *New York Times* (17 April).

Nizer, Louis, date unknown. How about low-cost drugs for addicts? Obtained from American Civil Liberties Union files.

Ostrowski, James. 1989. Thinking about drug legalization. Policy analysis #121 for CATO Institute (25 May).

————. 1988. Why cocaine and heroin should be decriminalized. Advisory report of the Committee on Law Reform. Unpublished paper. New York County Lawyers Association.

Pear, Robert. 1989. U.S. praises Haitians on drug efforts. *New York Times* (1 April).

Pillard, Nina. 1989. Drug Testing. *Civil Liberties* (Winter):4.

Pitt, David E. 1988. Dealers return to streets police swept in Queens. *New York Times* (5 December).

———. 1989. Drug cases clog New York City courts. *New York Times* (4 April).

Pooley, Eric. 1989. A federal case. *New York* (27 March):49–58.

———. 1989. Fighting back against crack. *New York* (23 January):30–40.

Rangel, Charles B. 1988. Legalize drugs, not on your life. *New York Times* (17 May).

Reuter, Peter. 1988. Can the borders be sealed? *Public Interest* (Summer).

Riding, Alan. 1989. Colombian cocaine dealers top European market. *New York Times* (29 April).

———. 1988. Drug lords acquire Colombian ranches and win new allies. *New York Times* (21 December).

———. 1988. Western panel is asking end to all curbs on drug traffic. *New York Times* (2 February).

Rimer, Sara. 1989. Homeless men find drug-free zone amid chaos in a shelter. *New York Times* (22 April).

Robbins, William. 1988. Armed, sophisticated and violent, two drug gangs blanket nations. *New York Times* (25 November).

Roberts, Albert R. 1988. Substance abuse among men who batter their mates. *Journal of Substance Abuse* (5):83–87.

Rosecan, Jeffrey S., M.D. 1988. Hair testing not valid for cocaine abuse. Letter to the Editor. *New York Times* (31 October).

Savage, David G. 1989. High court OKs drug tests for some workers. *Cleveland Plain Dealer* (22 March).

Schmalz, Jeffrey. 1988. Bank is charged by U.S. with money-laundering. *New York Times* (12 October).

———. 1989. One citizen's lone War on Drugs: A lonely fight, then death. *New York Times* (24 March).

Schur, Edwin M., and Hugo Adam Bedau. 1974. *Victimless Crimes*. Englewood Cliffs, N.J.: Prentice-Hall.

Sciolino, Elaine. 1989. Production rising worldwide, State Dept. says. *New York Times* (2 March).

Sherman, Lawrence W. 1989. The drug battle doesn't need martyrs. *New York Times* (16 August).

Slaughter in the streets. 1988. *Time* (5 December):32.

Smith, Philip. 1988. The soldier's story: People in the trenches speak out against the War on Drugs. *Reason* (August/September):31–33.

Stiteler, Rowland. 1988. High finance: Why every drug dealer needs a personal banker. *Orlando Sentinel Sunday Magazine* (4 December).

Stoll, Suzanne Marcus. 1985. Why not heroin? The controversy surrounding the legalization of heroin for therapeutic purposes. *Journal of Contemporary Health, Law and Policy* (Spring):173–194.

Sullivan, Ronald. 1989. U.S. agency lists Jamaicans thought to be in drug gangs. *New York Times* (6 April).

Szulc, Tad. 1989. Join with Castro to fight drugs. *New York Times* (9 August).

Terry, Don. 1989. Bystander, 12, is shot and killed in drug dispute. *New York Times* (22 January).

———. 1989. Drug riches of the Capital luring poor youth down a bloody path. *New York Times* (31 March).

3 former drug agents charged in fraud scheme. 1988. *New York Times* (25 November).

33 Charged with laundering $500 million in drug profits. 1989. *New York Times* (23 February).

Tolchin, Martin. 1989. The government still waits to test millions for drugs. *New York Times* (26 March).

Toufexis, Anastasia. 1989. A not-so-happy anniversary. *Time* (23 January):54.

Trainor, Bernard E. 1989. Military's widening anti-drug role. *New York Times* (27 August).

Treaster, Joseph B. 1989. Colombia welcomes U.S. aid but foresees a long struggle. *New York Times* (27 August).

———. 1989. Cuba says it wants to help on drugs. *New York Times* (26 July).

Trebach, Arnold. 1987. *The great Drug War.* New York: Macmillan.

———. 1982. *The heroin solution.* New Haven: Yale University Press.

Turque, Bill, Robert Parry, and Erik Calonius. 1989. Hitting the drug lords. *Newsweek* (4 September):18–24.

Two charged on Long Island in a money-laundering case. 1989. *New York Times* (27 August).

250 in court cheer as killer of officer gets 25 years to life. 1989. *New York Times* (17 May).

Uhlig, Mark A. 1989. Drug Wars: U.S. weighs a military escalation. *New York Times* (9 July).

U.N. accord on drug trafficking is signed. 1988. *New York Times* (21 December).

U.S. Department of Justice. Bureau of Justice Statistics Special Reports. 1989. *Correctional Populations in the United States, 1986.*

———. 1988. *Drug Law Violators, 1980–86.* (June).

———. 1988. *Drug Use and Crime* (July).

―――. 1989. *Felony Sentences in State Courts, 1986* (February).

―――. 1983. *Prisoners and Drugs* (March).

―――. 1988. *Profile of State Prison Inmates, 1986* (January).

―――. 1988. *Report to the Nation on Crime and Justice* (March).

U.S. Department of Justice, Drug Enforcement Administration. 1987. *Controlled Substances Act as amended to May 1, 1987.*

―――. 1988. *Drugs of Abuse.*

U.S. General Accounting Office, 1988. *Controlling drug abuse: A status report.*

―――. 1987. *Strategic defense initiative program* (November).

―――. 1988. *Drug control: Issues surrounding increased use of the military in drug interdiction* (April).

―――. 1988. *Drug control: U.S. international narcotics control activities* (March).

―――. 1988. *The National Narcotics Intelligence Consumers Committee Report, 1987* (April).

U.S. plots death by herbicide for hardy coca plants. 1988. *Cleveland Plain Dealer* (16 September).

Van den Haag, Ernest. 1985. Legalize those drugs we can't control. *Wall Street Journal* (8 August).

Wade, Betsy. 1989. Knowing the rules of the road wherever you are. *New York Times* (19 March).

Warner, John. 1983. International programs. *Drug Enforcement* (Fall):27–30.

Weiner, Eric. 1989. Airborne drug is at a stalemate. *New York Times* (30 July).

Weinraub, Bernard. 1989. Money Bush wants for drug war is less than sought by Congress. *New York Times* (30 January).

Wilkerson, Isabel. 1989. Crack and gunfire come to a quiet place. *New York Times* (9 January).

―――. 1988. Detroit crack empire showed all earmarks of big business. *New York Times* (18 December).

Williams, Terry. 1989. *The Cocaine Kids.* Reading, Mass.: Addison-Wesley.

Willis, David K. 1984. The debate on legalizing narcotic drugs grinds on. *Christian Science Publishing Society* (11 April).

Wines, Michael. 1989. Polls find public favors tougher laws against drug sale and use. *New York Times* (15 August).

Wisotsky, Steven. The drug crackdown: Trashing the Bill of Rights. Unpublished essay that expands on ideas advanced in Steven Wisotsky's *Breaking the impasses in the war on drugs* (Westport Conn.: Greenwood Press, 1986).

————, Lester Grinspoon, John Kaplan, Leon B. Kellner, Mark A. R. Kleinman, David A. J. Richards, Thomas Szasz, M.D., and Norman E. Zinberg, M.D. 1987. War on Drugs: A symposium. *Nova Law Review* (Spring):891–1052.

Wolff, Craig. 1988. As Hartford drug trade rises, so does violence. *New York Times* (17 December).

Zimmerman, Leroy. 1988. A war for the hearts and minds of our children. *New York Times* (31 March).

FOR FURTHER READING

Boaz, David. 1988. The legalization of drugs: Decriminalization. *Vital Speeches* (15 August).

Church, George. 1988. Should drugs be made legal? *Time* (30 May):12–19.

Courtwright, David T. 1982. *Dark Paradise: Opiate Addiction in America before 1940*. Cambridge, Mass.: Harvard University Press.

Grauer, Neil A. 1988. *Drugs and the Law*. New York: Chelsea House.

Hamill, Peter. 1988. "Facing up to drugs: Is legalization the solution? *New York* (15 August):20–27.

Kerr, Peter. 1988. The unspeakable is debated: Should drugs be legalized? *New York Times Magazine* (15 May).

Marshall, Elliot. 1988. *Legalization: A Debate*. New York: Chelsea House.

Mondzac, Allen M., M.D. 1984. In defense of the reintroduction of heroin into American medical practice and H.R. 5290: The Compassionate Pain Relief Act. *New England Journal of Medicine* (23 August).

Musto, David F., M.D. 1987. *The American Disease: Origins of Narcotic Control*. New York: Oxford University Press.

Nadelan, Ethan. 1988. U.S. drug policy: A bad export. *Foreign Policy* (Spring):83–108.

A national town meeting: The legalization of drugs. 1988. *The Koppel Report*. Transcript (13 September).

Stoll, Suzanne Marcus. 1985. Why not heroin? The controversy surrounding the legalization of heroin for therapeutic purposes. *Journal of Contemporary Health, Law and Policy* (Spring):173–194.

153

INDEX

154

155

157

158

ABOUT THE AUTHOR

Susan Neiburg Terkel grew up in Lansdale, Pennsylvania, and was educated at Cornell University, where she studied child development and family relationships. She has published several books for children including *Yoga Is for Me, Abortion: Facing the Issues,* and *Feeling Safe, Feeling Strong: How to Prevent Sexual Abuse and What to Do If It Happens to You,* which she coauthored with Janice Rench. She lives in Hudson, Ohio, with her husband and three children.